Prescription for Change

for

doctors who want a life

by

Susan E. Kersley

MB BCh   MEd   BA

Runnelstone books

Published in the UK by Runnelstone Books
©Susan E. Kersley 2003

First published 2003

British Library of Cataloguing-in-Publication Data
A catalogue entry for this book is available from the British Library

ISBN 0-9545863-0-1

Printed and bound by R. Booth Ltd, Cornwall, UK

Cover photograph ©Jonathan B Kersley

$$\boxed{\mathbf{R_{\!x}}}$$

CONTENTS

PART ONE

You can change your life

What we call the beginning is often the end. And to make an end is to make a beginning. The end is where we start from.
T. S. Eliot

Chapter 1: Life Coaching and doctors

What would make your life better?

Could it be any or all of the following?

- improved communication skills
- better relationships
- more effective use of time
- better self-care
- a clear focus on what is important for you
- an understanding and application of boundaries
- giving and receiving support
- more balance between work and home life
- happiness
- feeling valued

If you know something is missing in your life[1] and want the opportunity to reflect on your medical career and change the way you deal with challenges then Life Coaching, which is for successful people, may be for you.

Like many doctors you may be unhappy,[2] especially if you believe you are overworked, underpaid, inadequately supported, have falling status, are worn out by change, have less control over what you do and are increasingly accountable.[3]   The Health Service is deteriorating as politicians raise patients' expectations of what is possible.[4] As you become more harassed the quality of your patient care might be affected.[5]

Does life as a doctor have to be like this?

Life Coaching offers you support, discussion, encouragement and

1 BMJ Career Focus, 8 April 2000, Atik, Yaacov, Personal Coaching for senior doctors
2 BMJ 5 May 2001, 1078 Survey result; 1073,Smith, Richard, Editorial, Why are doctors so unhappy?
3 BMJ 19 May 2001, 1197 Ferriman Annabel, Doctors explain their unhappiness
4 BMJ 19 May 2001 1197 Kmietowicz, Zosla, GP dossier
5 BMJ 14 November 1998, 1335, Firth-Cozens, Jenny, Hours, sleep, teamwork and stress

motivation enabling you to deal better with the strain of being a doctor. By developing enhanced relationship and communication skills[6] the way you deal with difficult colleagues or patients can be improved. Coaching provides you with the chance to re-think what you value in your life. A Life Coach is there for you, encourages you to follow your own agenda and gives you the opportunity to talk to someone who listens fully to you. This can provide a new perspective on a situation. A challenging question or two may strike a chord, help you recognise patterns in your life and decide how to change them. The process can empower and motivate you. When you recognise and satisfy your own needs you become even better at what you do, which is important for coping with the ups and downs of life.[7] Coaching opens your eyes to parts of life which you have neglected and encourages you to introduce new habits to improve your fulfilment in areas unconnected with work.

If you are experiencing the frustration, stress, low morale, disempowerment and overwork of being a doctor, this may become detrimental to you, your wellbeing and the health of your patients.[8] [9] When you are fit emotionally and physically, you and also your patients benefit.

A Life Coach listens, reflects and encourages you to set and reach your goals, by helping you focus on specific actions and steps. Rather like a sports trainer to a champion, a Life Coach encourages you to go that little bit further than you would on your own.

How does Life Coaching differ from counselling?

Life Coaching is a forward looking, active process, whereas counselling tends to deal with and explore emotional issues from the past and cope with crises. Life Coaching is about improving the quality of your life and creating what you want in it now and for the future. It enables you to close the gap between how your life is and how you would like it to be. It

6 Hospital Doctor, 24 May 2001, 11, Camm, John, Why bad teams make you ill
7 BMJ 12 December 1998 1608, Stewart-Brown, Sarah Emotional well-being and its relation to health
8 BMA News, May 19 2001, Wafer, Alex, Waiting list pressures put doctors health in danger
9 BMA News Review, April 11 1998,36, Williams, Kate, Coping with work stress.

encompasses all areas of life, not only your career.

The medical model

You are used to patients with unrealistic expectations of what you can do. The traditional model is of the doctor with all the answers, able to cure everyone and everything.

This misconception by your patients, and possibly believed by you too, includes the belief that you are superhuman and cannot possibly have any health problems yourself. Sadly this is not the case and doctors may find it difficult to deal with their own mental or physical illnesses and recognise their own needs. [10] [11]

As a frustrated GP or doctor working in hospital or the community you are likely to be part of a multidisciplinary health care team so the way patients are treated is often arranged to fit around reaching the latest Government targets, (such as reduction of numbers on the waiting list), which may or may not be related to clinical need. Managers have the final say about much of what you do, and you might not have been part of the decision making process.[12] You may be fed up about being at the mercy of a system which you believe you have to put up with because it can't be changed.

The coaching model

In an ideal world you could work and co-operate well with colleagues and managers, listen to each other and recognise that everyone involved has something to contribute. Every member of the team would respect and value each other. Your medical skills would be used appropriately and non-medical tasks delegated correctly to others trained to do them efficiently. You would learn new skills regularly to keep up to date and work even more professionally. Moreover, you would have the time and energy to have a happy and fulfilling life outside work, since you are clear about setting and

10 BMJ Career Focus, 12 May 2001, Baron, Susannah, Doctors who have chronic illnesses
11 The Times, 6 July 2000, Ahuja, Anjana, Doctors in despair
12 Hospital Doctor, 5 April 2001, Bratby, Lisa, Survey shows pressure A&E doctors are under

maintaining boundaries and have excellent communication skills with patients, colleagues and managers.

Women doctors

Women doctors have twice the rate of suicide of other women[13]. In spite of opportunities for job sharing and part time appointments, full time colleagues may resent this.[14] There are now more women than men qualifying in medicine. The culture of the medical profession is slowly recognising this.

If you are a female doctor you have added stress possibly in relation to:

- a desire to succeed in your chosen speciality while being aware of your biological clock and worrying about the ideal time to have children[15]
- coming to terms with not having any children
- if you have children - concerns about adequate childcare

However well organised there may be problems such as having to stay with a patient knowing that your child is waiting to be collected from school.

Medicine, like being a parent, can be an all-encompassing way of life, not just a job. You may be involved in looking after everyone else's needs while neglecting your own.

Life Coaching: is it for doctors?

It is widely understood that there is low morale and frustration amongst doctors in the NHS. The word '*doctor*' seems to be permanently linked to the word '*stress*'. There are harassed consultants and GPs[16] buckling under the strain.

---

13 The Independent on Sunday, 13 May 2001, Harper, Victoria, Operating under Pressure
14 Hospital Doctor, 19 April 2001, Grant, Sarah, The battle for flexible work.
15 Hospital Doctor, 5 April 2001, Thompson, Audrey, When is the best time to have children?
16 BMA News, May 19 2001, Clews, Graham, BMA dossier paints a stark picture of overworked GPs

Life Coaching promotes the advantages of looking after your physical and emotional needs. It encourages you to have better balance and fulfilment in all areas of your life. When you work with a coach you learn to say '*no*' more often and set clearer boundaries, both physical and emotional. By getting rid of whatever drains your energy and increasing the things which give you more '*get-up-and-go*', your life as a doctor can be much improved[17].

What would make your life as a doctor more bearable?[18]

- being valued more
- more money
- professional support network
- more time
- less paperwork
- less isolation
- being able to express early grievances
- constructive peer review
- more sleep
- an opportunity to express and deal with anger
- collaboration and communication of team members

Coaching is your ***prescription for change*** to achieve all of these.

17 Ontario Medical Review, November1999-April 2000, Kaufmann, M, The 12-steps for physicians who seek rehumanizing.
18 BMJ Career Focus 28 October 2000, Luck, Carole, Reducing stress among junior doctors

Chapter 2: Are you ready?

Life is what happens to you while you're busy making other plans.
John Lennon

Can you have a life and be a doctor too?

How would you like to lead a happy and fulfilled life with plenty of time for everything? Can you imagine what it would be like to be naturally tired after a satisfactory day's work, to have enough energy when you go home to spend quality time with your family and be able to look after your body, mind and spirit on a regular and enjoyable basis? Is this an impossible dream?

When you are on a treadmill of un-relenting work from demanding patients and Government quotas, do you sometimes wonder how you will get through another day?

Has the golden dream become tarnished?

Have you resigned yourself to the never ending pressure of being a doctor and decided to put up with the erosion of work into your personal life? Did you work hard for so many years for this?

What is so special about being a doctor?

There is no doubt that medicine is a very fulfilling and satisfying profession. But does being a doctor prevent you from fully enjoying your family, your partner and taking an active part of your community? Does it stop you looking beyond your medical role towards your own personal, emotional and spiritual needs? Does your inability to 'switch off' relate to a need in you to feel wanted and important?

Does the challenge of sorting out problems, making decisions, arranging appropriate investigations and initiating the right treatment blur the reality of not being valued, your lack of personal choice and the inevitability of long hours of frustration?

As a doctor, you spend most of your time caring for others and may, as a result, neglect looking after your own general health and well being. Has your physical or emotional health suffered as a result of the demands made of you? Do you wish you had the courage to say *'enough is enough'* because you know, deep down, that you would be able to live a better life? Is the possible response of others keeping you doing things you no longer want to do? Are you waiting for someone else to initiate change? If so, you may wait a long time. Sometimes the only way things can be different is for you, as an individual, to take some action.

Prescription for change

Now is the time for you to find your own ***prescription for change*** so that you can be a doctor and have a life too. You won't find what you are looking for on a pharmacy shelf but, if you are ready, this book will guide you with signposts and tools. If you read it with an open mind and consider other possibilities then you will discover what you search.

What's stopping you doing what you want?

It may be fear, lack of clarity about your desired outcome, or not knowing how to convert your dreams into achievable goals. Be prepared to look at your beliefs objectively and be creative in your thinking. It's called *'getting out of the box'*. The instructions for getting out of the box are written on the outside. In other words when you look at your world from another perspective, you will know what you have to do.

This book is the catalyst for the life you want

If you are clear about what you want to achieve then you have to find the right map to reach your destination. You have a choice right now. You can continue the way you are and be fulfilled medically while you neglect the rest. However, if you dream of a better life then this book could be a beginning of a new journey. You can choose to take action or do nothing. What will you do?

I'll ask you to think about your life. Some of the questions may challenge you or start you thinking. Some will have an obvious answer, others may take a while for you to consider. The questions are there to encourage you to reflect on your life, how you'd like it to be and how making changes in the way you deal with a situation can make a difference. It's very easy to sit back and resign yourself to what is, rather than what could be, the *'I've made my bed, now I have to sleep in it'* mentality. Instead of complaining about the 'system' you could start to believe that you **can** make a difference.

Recording your journey

It may be useful to jot things down in a special notebook, a journal, and keep a personal record of the ups and downs of your life's journey. Over the next few weeks there will be times which seem very difficult, when you feel as though you are being tossed about in a storm and wonder if you've made a big mistake to even think about making changes. Writing your own account of what's happening to you will help to keep your focus on your ultimate destination and guide yourself into calmer waters to proceed to it.

Are you ready to start?

The first step to getting the things you want out of life is this: decide what you want. Ben Stein

Take a moment and imagine your ideal life. Think about the sights, the smells, the sounds and how you feel. Close your eyes and see it all in glorious Technicolor. Would you like to be there instead of here? Don't worry if you have no idea at this stage how you can reach this life; you are on your way. If you have a vision or some ideas then the next thing is to get on to the right path. Break big goals into smaller steps that you can begin today. You've already taken the first step by recognising that you would like things to be different and imagining specifically what it is you want instead. Well done! Too many people put up with an unsatisfactory life believing it is their 'lot,' and their fleeting ideas are dismissed as impossible.

Dr A would like to be a photographer instead of a GP. He wants to gain a professional qualification. He must find out what courses are available. So the very first step is to make a phone call to the local college. He does this and asks for an application form. He's on his way towards his goal!

Life has its ups and downs

Not everything is the way you want it to be. There is always a lesson to be learned from adversity. Try it. If you have particularly difficult day, ask yourself:

- what have I learned from this experience?
- what positive can I find amongst the negative?
- if I were ever to find myself in that situation again what would I do differently?

Notice your thoughts and begin to foster a more positive mindset.

Dr B was exhausted because of visiting his dying father each week. The positive things were that he spent more quality time with his mother than he had for years and was happy to be able to give her the support she needed. He also realised how nice it was to have a few hours each week to catch up on some medical journal reading on the train journey to London and back.

As you explore the various options to find your own ***Prescription for change*** take time to think about anything which resonates with you. There may be a reason for the 'gut feeling' you get from a particular example or quotation. Explore those things more fully and notice where the thoughts lead you.

However brilliant your ideas, your life will not change unless you do something you are not doing now. It's a well known adage that if you continue to do what you've always done you will continue to get what you've always got.

I encourage you to find someone to support you: a mentor, coach, friend or colleague, someone who inspires and motivates you to continue when you feel stuck and be a sounding board. Who is there for you?

Your journey

Like any expedition, life's journey is not always plain sailing or comfortable. There may be times when you are filled with doubt and wonder whether you've made a big mistake. Keep your mind open to different possibilities and take advantage of the opportunities you find. Even though you may have a bit of a rough crossing with pressure from friends, family or colleagues who do not understand, think you have lost your way and try to get you back on the track you were on before. If you hang on and keep your ultimate goal clearly in your mind, then eventually the storm will settle and you will reach your destination. Be aware of possible hazards so you can ride the storm. Remember there is likely to be some sense of chaos on the way to your ideal life.

Are you are ready to think about your life?

There is no such thing as a long piece of work, except one that you dare not start. Charles Baudelaire

Chapter 3: Do you have a life?

Doctor's lives

Recently I talked to several doctors about their lives. To my surprise there were two distinct responses.
There were those angry because they felt

- undervalued
- overworked
- underpaid

They complained bitterly about

- not having enough time
- working with colleagues and partners with whom they found it difficult to communicate

They were frustrated by

- lack of understanding of their role
- unsatisfactory working relationships

They found it difficult to maintain a happy home life when demands of their patients have to be dealt with as a priority.[19]

I heard too from doctors who neglected their own health and well-being and were unable to follow the advice they would give their patients.

Do you recognise yourself?

A female general practitioner knows her children are waiting to be collected from school while she deals with a suspected heart attack in the surgery.

19 Smith R. Why are doctors so unhappy? BMJ 2001;322: 1078

Another general practitioner continues to work doing surgeries when she is ill herself because there is no one else to do the work. She is frustrated that a large proportion of the patients come for non-medical reasons. Perhaps as a result of not looking after herself and taking time off when she is ill, she feels unwell and tired for several weeks afterwards.

A hospital consultant sees too many patients during an outpatient clinic because of Government targets.

Life as a doctor

As a result of the lifestyle that many doctors lead and the unrealistic expectations patients have of them, there is a high level of stress in the profession and doctors' health is suffering.[20]

When you arrive at your clinic or surgery do you inwardly groan when you pick up the notes and recognise another of your 'heart-sink' patients waiting to see you? You know you have to reach certain targets each month and find it frustrating that many of these are unrelated to clinical need. Both your physical and emotional health are affected by your lifestyle. If you were your own doctor you would say that it can't go on like this, the time has come to take yourself in hand, pull yourself together and make some changes.

So why do you continue to put up with the way things are?[21] Making changes seems difficult to do and you may decide it's easier to keep things the same.

But is this a life?

Have you forgotten why you became a doctor? What happened to the ideals you had when you went to medical school? How have you come to terms with the demands of the patients and the system? Would you like to connect again with the values that are important to you? Can you balance how you'd

20 Stewart-Brown S. Emotional well-being and its relation to health. BMJ 1998; 319: 1608
21 Clark S. Why do people become doctors and what can go wrong? BMJ 2000; 320

like your life to be with the reality of working in the NHS?

The other side of the picture

There are other doctors who aren't fed up. If you are in this group, you are content, fulfilled, lead a happy life and may be wondering what this chapter is about. Even though you are busy, you know how to 'switch off' so you relax, have fun, plenty of time with your family and friends, and also time to pursue your own interests and hobbies. I'd like to congratulate you and ask you to support your colleagues to live the same way.

How do the two groups differ?

How do members of the second group manage to have a good quality of life? What do they do   which eludes the first group? Their secret seems to be that they:

- are very clear about boundaries, particularly between work and leisure
- work hard and then switch off and go home
- have an interest or hobby, often creative or sports orientated
- are excellent time managers
- are clear about how they spend their day
- know what to do and what to delegate
- don't waste time
- have excellent communication skills
- look after themselves physically and emotionally[22]

Is it difficult to change?

The way you live now has some stability. Even if you aren't happy you know the rules and you live in your comfort zone. To introduce a new way of doing something may take a few weeks of being self-conscious before it

---

22 Gray C. Life, your career and the pursuit of happiness BMJ 1997; 317

becomes automatic. The first time you try something different your actions may seem contrived and uncomfortable, but eventually you will develop a habit and your comfort zone increases. Isn't it worth enduring a little awkwardness to make a big difference to the rest of your life? Do you recall how ill at ease and difficult it was to remember all the actions you needed to drive a car? It's the same with life. At first making changes seems easier said than done until eventually you get into your 'autopilot' and make them without thinking. It's too easy to stay in an unsatisfactory situation unless you have the strong desire to get out of it and are prepared to do something.

How do you change the system?

By changing what **you** do. You can't change other people, only yourself. Because everything is interconnected, when you do something different, others will change too. Don't wait for them. Be proactive and take the first step.[23]

How can you start?

Decide what you want to achieve. Begin with the end in mind. Be very specific about your goal. For example '*I want to feel less stressed*' is vague. A specific goal could be '*I want to see a maximum of 15 patients in my outpatient clinic by the end of December.*' Even though at first it may seem to be something totally impossible, is your goal theoretically achievable? Decide on the date by when you want to achieve your goal and write it in your diary. Take the first step. This means you have to make a definite commitment, an undertaking to do something that you are not doing now. What will you commit to doing by the end of this month? By the end of this week? By the end of today?

Do you want to see fewer patients? Do you put up with overbooking week after week? Have you thought of asking the appointments clerk to book one less patient per clinic each week? That would be four less per month, each month. In nine months you could go from 48 patients to 12 per clinic. (see also Chapter 17)

23 Covey S. *The seven habits of highly effective people* New York: Simon and Schuster, 1989

What's stopping you?

Fear is the most common reason for not doing something. Fear that it might not work; fear of what other people will say about you; fear about making a fool of yourself. The thought of challenging the system is scary. If you are worried that your manager would lose his or her job, think instead about how you are perpetuating an unsatisfactory system. If the system needs to be changed it can be done by individuals making their own small changes. Are you letting fear stop you making progress? Would you prefer to continue as you are because of it? What might happen if your fear materialised? How does that compare with what will happen if you continue as you are? What are the advantages of making the changes you want?

Top 10 benefits from making changes

1. When you start to change one part of your life other parts change too
2. You have more time
3. You stop procrastinating
4. You spend some time each day doing something for yourself
5. You get rid of things which drain energy
6. You enjoy more satisfactory relationships
7. You understand and create your boundaries
8. You look after yourself
9. You know what really matters in your life
10. You take action, instead of waiting for others

How can you make a start?

Some people have their own reasons for keeping things as they are and they enjoy telling you all the negative outcomes, as they see them, of what you plan to do. Once you've made a start it's easier to continue. So, having made the decision to change it's important that you:

- do **something**
- **start** with a small step

- find someone to **motivate and encourage** you

When is the best time?

The best time is **now**. It's easy to think of reasons why it would be better to postpone the decision. Do a reality check to make sure there are genuine reasons for delaying or whether your own beliefs are stopping you. Too often you have good ideas and you even tell others what you've decided and then do nothing. Don't procrastinate any longer. It's making a start that is so important. You don't have to wait for a whole day to complete the task. There is something empowering about making a start and doing a little bit each day.

Why is there a need for change?

Many doctors believe they have to deal with whatever the system throws at them. Some leave medicine entirely, a few seek jobs to do part time, others continue until they reach breaking point, take an overdose or take time off for stress related illnesses. If you want your life to be better, happier and less stressful, it's a sign of your strength not weakness to talk about and get support to achieve what you want. Don't wait until you can't cope any more. You need lots of energy to make changes.

But nothing changes

Unless you take **personal responsibility** then nothing may change. If you wait for someone else then you may be disappointed. The system takes many years to alter but you can begin to enjoy your own life much, much more if you decide what you'd like and take action.

Imagine a miracle

Close your eyes for a moment and see yourself in your ideal life. How do you feel? From your dream for the future decide on something you can do **now** to move you nearer towards what you want.

Then start with the first step. **Today**.

Chapter 4: Are you a round peg in a square hole?

This above all: to thine own self be true. William Shakespeare

But how can it be?

If the thought of the day ahead fills you with dread and you have that *'Monday morning feeling'* every day then, even though you are doctor, a pillar of the community, following a worthy profession, you may not be living the life you want. You may wonder how or why you are so disheartened and unhappy about the decision you made to become a doctor. Thoughts about whether you've picked the right specialty or even career[24] can make you insecure and anxious.

Did you make the wrong choice?

Studying medicine and becoming a doctor was a major decision in your life. Were your motives for entering the profession misguided? Do you regret your chosen career, wish you were happier with it but believe that there's nothing you could change?

What can you do?

Take an objective look at where you are. Don't linger too long in misgivings or examining what might have been. The past can't be changed, it made you the person you are today. You may have already spent a lot of time going over and over what happened, the how and the why of it all. But eventually the time comes when you have to look to your future. Will it be the opportunity you want? If you are prepared to do something to alter the course you are on then you can look forward to a better life.

Dr A did medicine to spite a teacher who said he wasn't clever.

Dr B chose radiology, which she doesn't enjoy, instead of her passion

24 Dosani S. Stop the rotation I want to get off. *BMJ* 2002; 324

orthopaedics, because she was told surgery would be too difficult.

Then what?

Turn your mind's eye to what is yet to come and create a mental picture of what your life could be. Be very clear about what is important to you.[25]

Think about when you last felt that everything was going well for you, when life seemed effortless, you were confident and going with the flow. Then explore how you can have more of those feelings brought into your life again, both in and out of work.

Who are you?

You are a doctor, but what or who else are you without the 'doctor' label? Take a look at what's left without it. Is anyone there, or has the rest of you disintegrated like the wicked witch in the *Wizard of Oz*? What is unique and special about you? Your medical hat may be so much part of you that you may not be able to take it off very often. It may be stuck with superglue.

Since working is such an important part of your life it is vital to find ways to combine it with your hopes and values so that you are content, happy and fulfilled both inside and outside your job. You might wonder who you would be if a decision to leave medicine was forced on you, if you had to take early retirement on the grounds of ill health, for example. You are so busy with your work related activities that you have no time for anything else in your already stressful life. Your colleagues are little help as there is a culture of *'grin and bear it'* and *'why worry about things which may never happen'* But you **do** worry and a major concern is the answer to the question: *'Who am I?'*

What do you need to complete your personal jigsaw?

Have you forgotten who you really are? You are a doctor, full stop. So much

25 Houghton A. Values? What values? *BMJ* 2002; 324 S59

so that sometimes you find yourself wondering who you are without the label, and who you would be if you decided to leave medicine. Sometimes you feel almost invisible, as though others only see your white coat and stethoscope.

You need to find the missing piece before you reveal the jigsaw. Where does it fit? Where is it hidden? When you introduce yourself to someone you've just met, what do you tell them and what do you leave out? What does this say about you?

Is there something important about you that you hide, ration the truth about, or choose to keep as a secret?

Dr C entered the same specialty as her father but found it almost impossible to live up to his expectations.

Dr D never told his colleagues that he used to be a priest.

Dr E avoided telling his colleagues about his episodes of mental health problems.

Dr F dreaded anyone finding out that he had a partner of the same sex.

What do you want to tell?

Do you have a lack of clarity about your personal identity? Does what you say about yourself give a sense of your values, of what you feel passionately about, or what you love to do? If you are in the wrong specialty or profession, if you are a square peg in a round hole, how can you be true to yourself?

What's stopping you being honest, first with yourself and then with others? What do you fear? What's the worst thing that could happen? Whose life are you living? What do you need to do to make yourself more comfortable with your life? Is it time to let your true self shine through?

Being seen

In parts of West Africa people greet and respond to each other by saying '*I am here*' to which the response is '*I see you*' I am amazed at the effect of someone saying they see me. It is much more powerful than '*How do you do?*' It reminds me of the greeting used in Nepal '*Namaste*', meaning '*the divine in me recognises the divine in you*'.

Can you recognise the person beyond the job, beyond the stereotype? When you see them as they really are they will begin to see the authentic you too.

Is it ever too late?

Yes or no. Whatever you believe is true. But if you are unhappy then any change, however small, will begin to make a difference to what you believe about yourself. When others perceive you differently, then they may change the way they behave towards you too (for better or worse).

Like a garden, what you want won't bloom overnight. You have to plant lots of seeds, tend them, and then be patient until eventually some of them blossom.

Dr G wonders about giving up medicine as he's always wanted to be an artist. He decides to continue to work as a locum general practitioner to earn enough while pursuing an art degree. He becomes happier and more self confident as he takes some positive steps. An unexpected outcome is that he enjoys the medical work much more and decides to do both in parallel.

Here is a challenge: next time someone says to you: '*tell me a bit about yourself,*' avoid saying, '*I'm a doctor*' as the first thing. Instead, start with telling what you value, what the most important thing is for you. Perhaps this will lead you towards a renewed sense of personal worth and heightened self esteem.

What seeds for change will you plant this week?

He who knows others is wise. He who knows himself is enlightened
Lao Tzu

Chapter 5: How to change your life in seven easy steps

If you don't like something, change it. If you can't change it, change your attitude. Don't complain   Maya Angelou

STEP ONE: DO YOU WANT CHANGE?

Have you had enough of being overworked, undervalued and not doing things you really would like to do? Who makes the rules in your life?

Do any of the following resonate with you?

- *wondering whether to retire instead of meeting targets*
- *wishing you had more time*
- *health is suffering*

Is your life governed by objectives which don't relate to what you want?

Would you like more autonomy? Do **you** make the decisions in your life? Are you spending so much time at work that you hardly ever see your children? Did you miss first steps, first words or other milestones? Do you need to be much better organised?

Do you look after your own needs? Be truthful. What small change do you need to introduce into your life, your week or your day to improve your health and well being? Even though there may not be an instant result, you have to start somewhere, with something. What's stopped you in the past? Is that a valid reason? Really? Does your fear of what people might say or think of you stop you doing something beneficial for yourself?

Consider the future, your future: do you stay stuck because you might upset someone by your action? Do you prefer to stay unhappy?

Before you begin it's very important to be sure that you **do** want to change, that you **really** want your life to be different. Making changes is often scary. You may have reassured yourself for years with phrases such as:

- *when the children have left home I'll......*
- *when I've lost weight I'll.......*
- *when I get the job I'll......*

What delaying tactics do **you** use? List them in your journal and decide how you will deal with them in the future. There is no need to wait. Wouldn't it be much more fun to start the life you want **now** rather than some undefined time in the future?

Is the change you are thinking about something that **you** really want? Are you listening to your **own** voice? Or is it someone else's plan for your life? Is your desire for change coming from your own enthusiasm or because of internal messages from a parent, partner, teacher or someone else? Are the ideas in your head from someone who told you the 'rules' for life from their perspective? Your circumstances have changed since then. Perhaps you are no longer single or have become so again. You may now have a young family or your children have grown up and moved away. Life changes. It's important to recognise how your life is now. Is what you want a '*choice*' or is it a '*should*'?

Sometimes it's easier to stay in your everyday discomfort than to move into '*new waters*'. For example it is well known that *some people become chronic invalids until the court case to grant them compensation is complete.* Recognise and reflect on the '*pay-off*' from not changing.

Are you a bit of a '*control freak*' and find it difficult to let people make their own decisions? Let go of trying to control others. Trust them to do whatever they need to do. This letting go allows you more energy to do what **you** want.

What scares you?

Do you **really** know how others will react to you? Are you stopping yourself doing what you want because you are convinced that so and so would be upset or offended? Ask yourself: if that person behaves as you believe, what would be the worst thing that could happen as a result?

Reflect on this: **you are responsible for yourself**. You can decide how to respond to your experiences. You always have a choice. You can choose whether to be angry or sad, happy or indifferent.

How do you feel if you look out of the window and it's raining? Are you sad as you wanted to do some gardening or happy because you have the opportunity to go to a museum?

Notice your reactions

If you are at a social event and moan that you have better things to do, notice what happens when you tell yourself you are enjoying yourself, how great it is to have the opportunity to meet such interesting people.

Become aware of how, when you change your thoughts, your behaviour changes too.

How do you answer the question **Do you want to change,** now?

If your answer is **yes** then continue with **Step two**.

STEP TWO: HOW WOULD YOU LIKE IT TO BE?

You are ready to take the next step. You've decided you really do want to make some changes but are not sure how to start. Stephen Covey says in his book '*The Seven Habits of Highly Effective People: Begin with the end in mind.* If you want to change your life, you have to develop a clear vision of how life would be if everything was as you want

Visualise

Sit quietly and close your eyes. Starting with your feet, relax your lower limbs. Then working your way through your body, relax your abdomen and your arms. Finally let your face and your head settle down. Your breathing will become slow and shallow. Then imagine opening a door into a wonderful place. Keep your eyes closed, take a look around and using all your senses, in your mind's eye, look and hear, smell and touch your surroundings. Be aware of your emotions. Once you are sure you have explored as much as you can of your vision, take a few deep breaths, and slowly open your eyes. Have a good stretch. Then take your notebook or journal and write about what you saw, heard, smelled, tasted and felt.

Visualisation is an important tool to assist change because it helps you realise what you want. If you regularly say '*I can't stand this any longer*' but fail to think what you want instead, it is much less likely that anything will change.

It's as though you went into a shop and asked for a map, any map. You would be confused if you were given a map of Birmingham when you were exploring Glasgow.

Getting what you want is to know specifically what you would like. It's not enough to say '*No more of this*'. You have to be able to state positively what you wish for: '*What I want now is...*'

If you could be transported into your vision, how would you behave? What would be different about you? What about the expression on your face, your posture and the way you move about? How would others realise that you were having the time of your life? What can you start doing now? How would your behaviour or your body language be if you were already living your ideal life?

If you find visualisation difficult there are other ways to define what you want:

- what is most important to you?
- what do you value most in life?
- how can you live in a way that recognises your values?

A consultant in an inner city hospital would love to live by the sea so that he can sail regularly. Although he's said this often to his colleagues and family over many years, he takes no action. Does he really want to change?

What scares him? Is he clear about the vision? What could he do? He has various choices:

Continue as now. What would life be like if he stays put and doesn't make any change? How will he feel when he retires and realises he is no longer well enough to do what he wants?

Fit the things he wants into his current life style. Perhaps he can't move to the sea but he could go sailing on one of the big reservoirs, or take regular holidays by the sea.

Decide to make a big change in his life and move to live on the coast. When he looks at the job adverts he finds there are suitable jobs available in coastal towns.

The last option   might seem so big and so scary that he ends up doing nothing. He may, on the other hand decide to follow his dream and take a first step by making some enquiries to find out if it would be practical to pursue it. Something like this might happen: he contacts various hospitals to enquire about job vacancies and looks in the BMJ each week for adverts for posts in areas he is interested in. He and his wife spend a weekend driving around the area and they talk about schools and house prices and what a move might mean for all of them. With this knowledge he can begin to make an informed choice.

Things happen when you have a clear vision.

Here are more examples of what some doctors would like to do.

A general practitioner wants to work part time so he can present television programmes. He hasn't done this because he thinks he is too old and would have to do a course for presenters too. So, he does nothing and life goes on as before. His beliefs stop him taking any action. His coach challenges him to make enquiries to find out some facts, about possible age barriers and qualifications needed. After he talks to some people he has greater clarity about the situation and applies to become a news reader on local radio. This is the first step towards the vision.

A pathologist always wanted to join a choir. He hasn't done so because he's much too busy. During coaching he is challenged about what he could do to create more time in order to join. He thinks about what doesn't have to be done by him (that he can delegate). He realises that filing patients' notes is the clerical officer's task not his. He also devises a more efficient system of dictating notes as he goes along. As a result he finishes on time and is able to go to the choir rehearsal.

That's the crux of it: you have to become clear about your vision for your future, be creative and let your ideas flow.

If you are a doctor there is nothing, except your own beliefs, stopping you finding time for whatever you are passionate about. There is plenty of room in your life to do more than you could possibly imagine. You might even find you began to enjoy the medical work much more when you take some time out, regularly, to do something which gives you joy.

What do you regret giving up?

Do you tell people about hobbies, activities, you used to do before you got so busy? Wouldn't you like to do those things again and regain some balance in your life, and look after your physical, mental and emotional health much more?

Do you love dancing, yoga, painting or playing the violin? Is it ages since you did any of these?

Stop talking and start doing. Start by day dreaming, thinking vividly about how it would be if you did some of the things you have given up on or put on hold for the time being. It's time to work out ways to do them again. With your vision in mind, you can start behaving *'as if'* what you want is already in your life.

Change your body language and you change the way you feel

If you want more confidence you can walk with your head up high. If you want to be happy, have a broad smile on your face.

Imagine feeling sad and depressed. Put your head downwards, round your shoulders, look to the ground. Does that make you feel even sadder? Then, stand up straight, with a big smile, shoulders back and striding out confidently. How do you feel now? Still feel depressed?

So this is step two: How would you like it to be? Have you got your vision clear?

Are you ready to move on to **Step three**?

STEP THREE: WHAT'S STOPPING YOU?

How your life is now compared with how you would like it to be?

Take a look at the possible obstacles in the way of having the life you want. It's easy to find excuses for not doing anything.

Your beliefs: If you are certain that jobs for doctors by the sea are oversubscribed then you don't send off for an application form.

Unproven assumptions: If you do something different this would upset other people. Are you so sure of what others would think or say if you did what you want to do? These ideas actually stop you doing what you want.

Check it out

Communicate. Ask for what you want. If the other person says '*Oh no you can't do that*' ask yourself '*what's the worst thing that can happen?*' Someone may react negatively to what you ask. They may be angry or jealous or sad. But that is **their** responsibility, not yours. Are you really not doing what you want because you worry that another person may be angry?

Take a risk every now and again

A consultant gynaecologist, who lives in a large house and whose children go to a private school, is worried what his colleagues would think if he moved away to live in the country and work in a district general hospital He realises that he would lose most of his private practice income and his wife wouldn't be able to wear designer clothes any more. But he's always wanted to live away from the city and own a smallholding. Suddenly he understands that it doesn't matter what his colleagues think of him and his children will be fine in the local school. His wife doesn't care if she wears jeans and a fleece as she plans to write a novel.

You may have a whole script of what various friends or colleagues would say or think about you if you did something they might find extra-ordinary. But if that is what you long to do, is it really out of character?

Could you instead believe that what you truly desire is absolutely **in** character, in contrast to the rest of the stuff, which bores you or causes your stress levels to rise.

What else is stopping you?

- deciding **how** to do it
- needing to learn some new skills
- wanting to gather more information before you proceed
- making a commitment to **when** you will do it

You've found out what may be stopping you, move on to **Step four**.

STEP FOUR: MAKE A START

However wonderful your plans and intentions, nothing will be different in your life unless you take some action. Think back to all the times you've decided something without doing anything. It doesn't get done, does it?

Are you making excuses, valid reasons to justify staying where you are? Do you believe that you can't do anything until:

- a new consultant is appointed
- another year or two
- the new ward has been built
- you are less busy

To make something happen, you have to make a start. Begin by letting the idea of change permeate inside you. Jot down as many ways you can think of as steps towards your goal. Some examples:

Make a telephone call to someone who may know the answers you seek

Dr X wonders how many nights on-call he will have in a particular job, so he phones the person currently doing the work. He is pleased to hear there is a night on-call service.

Look at job adverts.

Dr Y assumes that jobs by the sea 'never come up,' but when she starts to look through the BMJ each week there are suitable vacancies.

Use local facilities.

Dr Z has always wanted to join a band but has no idea if there is one nearby. He buys the local paper and looks at notices in the library, until he finds one not far away.

Dr A wants to meet people to form a walking group. She puts a card in the corner shop and soon finds some like minded people to walk with each weekend.

Make enquiries.

Dr B has put off learning Spanish because he's too busy. However, he finds that the adult education college has a course that he can attend during his free afternoon.

Dr G looks up Alaska on the internet and books the trip she's always wanted to do.

What will be your first step?

It could be something very small such as:

- make a few phone calls
- write a letter
- arrange to talk to someone who can give you an insight into what you want to do

But be wary: the other person has come from a different life experience. Listen and discuss with them but in the end the decision has to be yours, based on what you have found out about the subject and your own feelings.

Are you prepared to make a start? Then it's time to move to **Step five**.

STEP FIVE: DECISION TIME

Action

So, you've thought about what you **could** do, now decide what you **will** do. It's time to **make a plan**. Write down a list of the various stages you need to complete before you can get to where you want to go. For example: if you would love to do a part time course then until you find out where to do it, when the next course starts, how much it will cost and when you have to apply, then you will remain stuck.

Is what you want to do possible?

Make an informed decision. It's easy to dismiss something by saying '*I'm too old to apply for that'* or *'I wouldn't have the time for that'.* When you have the facts you have a basis to know if your idea is feasible or not. If you really want something, don't give up at the first hurdle, work out ways to overcome the challenges.

Stop making assumptions

Do you ever question your personal practice? Are you doing what you've always done? Is there a good reason for continuing in the same way? You may have done something for years and yet wasting time and energy on a procedure which has a dubious outcome, or which doesn't produce any worthwhile results. For example:

Should doctors wear white coats or not? Are the arguments for and against valid today? If not then consider other ways to achieve the same desired outcome.

Do you tell patients to return for follow up appointments, without considering whether you really need to see them regularly or could you ask them, instead, to contact you if certain signs or symptoms develop? There are routines for follow up appointments which are based on habit and have little basis on the patient's need or the doctor's time.

You may need to change your schedule, if you really want something that isn't in your life right now. Consider what is flexible, what can be stopped to free up time and facilitate the change you want.

Dr C decides to give up one hospital practitioner session He never enjoyed doing it and he knows he will have a more enjoyable time attending a ceramics class.

Dr D finds a trombone teacher for a weekly lesson instead of going to a boring meeting.

Don't limit yourself

Be open to other possibilities. Ask yourself, what other options are there?

Dr E buys a set of oil paints and an easel. She finds a distance learning course.

How much will it cost?

Do you make excuses based on the price? Can you quantify the value of living a life you love? How do you measure value in relation to money?

Dr F knows that flying lessons are expensive, but he wants to indulge himself and can afford to pay for them. The joy he gets as a result is immeasurable in monetary terms.

Who can support you?

Dr H wants to make changes and knows it will be easier to keep to his plan with the support of his colleagues. They arrange to be regularly accountable to each other.

Who do you have in your network to encourage you? Beware of people, with their own agenda, who don't want you to change because that will upset **their** lives. In an ideal supportive relationship you have someone who listens, motivates and challenges you to explore your options, persuades you to take action and celebrates your achievements This is more helpful than the person who tells you what to do, or is upset if you decide to do something different from their suggestion. Hiring a Life Coach is one way to have objective support.

You've made your decision to start and made a plan but still feel uncertain. Move on to **Step six.**

STEP SIX: INDECISION TIME

Suppose you are sure you've had enough of things as they are now but have not been able to visualise an alternative. What can you do? There are ways to make some space for the new ideas to flood in.

Take time to sit quietly, meditate, listen to music or go for a walk. Don't talk. Just allow whatever is in your subconscious to come into your conscious mind. Notice your thoughts. Don't edit anything but record your ideas in a notebook or a tape recorder. Be patient. The whole picture may be self-edited or dismissed too quickly. However ridiculous, there could be something useful.

Maybe you need to have a bit of a *'clear out'* both mentally and physically. They say that nature abhors a vacuum and so it seems to be. When you start to clear away your clutter, take it to the dump or put it into your *'mental shredder'* there will be a space for new ideas and opportunities.

Make a list of everything that gets on your nerves: preferably fifty or even a hundred items. Start with the easy things, and eliminate them one by one. It's a great feeling when you can cross things from your long list. Get them done; or ask someone else to do it, for pay or as a favour or as an exchange. As you do this, you may realise that some of the nagging things don't need to be done at all. Have you been keeping a broken toaster for years and know that it's cheaper to buy a new one rather than have it repaired?

Stop putting things off. Just do them as you see they need doing.

Throw away old journals and out of date things. Do you ever get around to reading the editions you missed? Be honest with yourself. What can you get rid of? Just do it!

Dr J throws away old medical journals and newspapers
Dr K gets rid of out of date pharmaceutical samples
Dr L arranges for a carpenter to build the shelves he needs
Dr M asks the receptionist with the loud voice to speak more quietly

Dr N asks that all patient files are put away at the end of the day

Taking action in areas unrelated directly to your goal provides space and energy for other things to change.
Move on now to **Step seven**.

STEP SEVEN: DO SOMETHING FOR YOURSELF

You are important. Very important. And sometimes it's good to do something special just for you. Reward yourself for what you've achieved this week. Celebrate the changes you've already begun to make. A special indulgence can be an incentive to get things done.

How will you treat yourself?

Here are some ideas:

- go for a walk
- have a hot bath
- go to the gym
- go out to a restaurant
- cook yourself a special meal
- see a good film
- sit quietly

What other ideas can you think of?

Doing something special for yourself is important to raise your self esteem, to value yourself and recognise that you've achieved something. It's easy to do things for other people most of the time and forget about your own needs. Now is the time to ask for what you want. Are you ready for the challenge?

Make a list of treats and incentives.
Make a commitment to nurture yourself.

The bonus

Everything is interconnected, so whatever changes you make will result in other things and people changing, too. You will be different and so will those around you. You can live a better life in which you are happy and fulfilled.

Never believe that a few caring people can't change the world. For, indeed, that's all who ever have. Margaret Mead

Chapter 6: How will you respond to your wake up call?

Opportunity is missed by most people because it is dressed in overalls and looks like work. Thomas A. Edison

Thinking about life

Have you had one of those landmark birthdays recently, the sort which makes you reflect on your life, look back over the years and wonder where they've gone? Have you become conscious of your own mortality and the realisation that you are not as young as you thought you were? The shock from recognising time passing and opportunities lost is a considerable one. Life is for living. But when you are part of a profession which encourages total immersion in work, so much so that medicine can be a lifestyle rather than a profession, you may have put off doing things *'until you are not so busy'* Are you waiting for some mythical time in the future? Will that time ever actually arrive?

When will you start to do what you want to achieve during your life?

Wake up

One day something happens to spur you into action. Something, totally unexpected and possibly rather sudden, which gives you a jolt and makes you decide the time has come to get moving on the things you plan to do with your life.

A middle-aged GP is overworked and stressed and would like to spend less hours in his practice. He recently found he has hypertension and started treatment. He would dearly like to move to a smaller house and drive a less expensive car but his wife won't agree to the changes. So he is committed to staying in the Practice until he is 65 because of his heavy financial commitments. He wishes he had done things differently. However after working with a coach he explores ways to change. He involves his wife in planning their future together.

Have you had a 'wake up call'?

Just like the shrill call of your alarm clock signalling the start of another day of overwork and stress, this is a *'get up and get going'* type of call. A persistent call that shakes your thoughts, resonates your conscience and asks the question, '*...if not now, when...*'

Perhaps you've had symptoms which mean you aren't quite as well as you thought you were. Maybe a friend or relative has a serious illness or died suddenly. Possibly you've discovered you have a disease you were unaware of until recently. Realistically you know that something has to change, things have to be different.

If so, then this is the time to rouse yourself, look at where you are in life and decide how you would really like it to be. Not only deciding but also working out how to do what you've made your mind up to do.

Whose life is it anyway?

Are you doing what someone else has decided is 'best' for you? Well meaning though they may be, other people may not really understand what matters to you. Sometimes your parents, your partner or your boss may have aspirations which don't seem right to you and yet there is a persistent inner voice telling you what you 'should' or 'shouldn't' do. Are you following someone else's path or one they wish they had followed?

Dr B never wanted to do medicine. She only did it to please her father who was a well known surgeon. She found the stress of living up to his reputation very difficult and in the end decided the only way to cope was to limit the times she saw her father. Following some coaching she realised that she could begin to communicate more effectively with him and make it clear that she was following her own path.

Look at your limiting beliefs

What are your reasons for doing or not doing something? When you say you want a different life, yet you never do anything about it ask: *'what is the worst thing that could happen if I did that?'* Listen to your answer and then ask again: *'so what if that happened...what is the worst thing that could happen as a result?'* If you limit yourself by a belief that you can't do something, ask *'why?'* Whatever your answer, keep asking yourself *'why?'* After about five 'whys' you will realise that the only thing stopping you is you.

Get out of your comfort zone

We all have things we feel secure about doing. In order to do something different we often have to step out of that comfort zone into a distinctly uncomfortable one. Don't expect that it will feel easy. You have to be prepared for some feelings of unease as you make changes. However, what happens as a result of taking a risk and doing something you expect to be difficult is that after a while the discomfort becomes less: your comfort zone increases in size and you have succeeded in making the changes you want.
How can you actually get on and do those things?

Become clear about what you will or won't put up with any more

Say 'no' more often. When you say 'no' what are you are saying 'yes' to?

Dr A says 'no' to seeing any pharmaceutical reps after 12 noon, so she says 'yes' to meeting a friend for lunch once a week.

Dr. B says 'no' to meetings in the evening, so he says 'yes' to communicating with his colleagues when he is less tired.

Look at the positives

A wake up call can be depressing and distressing. It may take over your life for a while. When you are in the midst of the crisis it can be difficult or even impossible to recognise anything positive from the experience. However, when the time is right for you and the clouds become less heavy, it may be useful to jot down your thoughts about the experience and what you've learned from it. You know very well what is worse, but try answering:

- *what is better?*
- *what insights have you had as a result of this experience about you and your life?*
- *what will you do differently as a result of your wake up call?*
- *when will you start?*

What are you waiting for?

You can make a choice. There is always a choice. You recognise the benefit of what happened for what it is: the chance to make a start, without further delay, to do what you want. Or you can ignore it completely. You can switch off the metaphorical buzzer in your head and heart. That's fine. The next call may be much louder and more insistent.

Have you ever set your clock and then felt cross when you found that you set it for the wrong time? It's difficult to go back to sleep when that happens, isn't it? Just like that, life's alarm bell tends to ring at what may seem to be the wrong time. However, instead of being cross about it, you can decide to recognise the opportunity it brings you to get things done, to try something new, or to complete something started but never finished.

If you imagine your life as a journey then your wake up call may be telling you it's time to change direction, change your plans too and head off to a different destination.

Even with these insights if you would like to benefit from your wake up call, the secret is to take action. Unless you do something differently then the opportunity passes by and nothing much changes. Look forward to what you can realistically achieve if you are aware that something major has changed in your life. Where would you like to go? What have you always wanted to try? There may be difficult times ahead. Unless you do something **now** then you won't even begin.

It will happen if you are willing

Keep your ears, eyes and mind open and look and listen for opportunities and ideas.

Jot down every idea you think of however weird or wonderful and pick one which appeals to you most. Think about it. Picture yourself achieving it. Imagine how you would feel. Then draw a mind-map, flow chart or list with small achievable steps you need to do to make the progress you want. Decide what you will do this month, this week, today. And then do it!

You will have responded to your wake up call and recognised it for what it is.

A remarkable opportunity. Don't let it pass you by.

The Chinese use two brush strokes to write the word 'crisis' One brush stroke stands for danger; the other for opportunity. In a crisis, be aware of the danger - but recognize the opportunity. Richard M. Nixon

PART TWO

Prescription for change

Change your thoughts and you change your world.
Norman Vincent Peale

Chapter 7: What would you do if you had the time?

Time is the coin of your life. It is the only coin you have, and only you can determine how it will be spent. Be careful lest you let other people spend it for you. Carl Sandburg

What would you do if you had all the time you need? You know that time is finite and you cannot have any more than 24 hours each day. Over a week there are 168 hours for you. If you deduct ten hours each day for sleeping and eating there are still 98 hours left! You **can** make a difference in your life; changes will happen if you are willing to consider ways to do things differently and are prepared to take some action. Shift some energy!

Dr A leaves his busy surgery and wonders where another day has gone. When he arrived the appointment list was already full and so was the waiting room. Before half an hour had passed, the receptionist brought in more sets of notes, and he felt a tension headache develop, which lasted until every patient left. The list of visits had grown by then. The woman who lives over the road won't have anything much wrong with her except a hangover. Meanwhile his own children are asleep in bed, and his wife is furious with him for being late again. He would dearly love to have more time for his family and for himself too. He would like to play squash again, but each day is the same. Whatever plans he makes have to be abandoned because he is so exhausted by the time he eventually gets home.

Are you frustrated about not getting things done? Do weeks go by when you never manage to find extra time for things you used to love to do before you got on the unending treadmill of overwork?

When did you last say: *'That was a fantastic day'* What's been lacking in your life over the last few years?

It's important to be clear about what you will do if you had extra time. Knowing this gives you an added incentive to free up time. By planning to do something very specific you will have a measure of whether or not you've been successful. What would you like to do again without feeling the pressure? Would you like to spend more hours with your partner, family and friends? Are you keen to be more involved in your community?

Make a list of all the things you want to do by the end of this year.

Write a date by each item by when you want to have done it. Month by month write what you need to do in order to reach your goal for the end of the year. For example: you've decided that you want to complete a certain project. That's fine. A good idea which is specific, measurable, achievable and realistic. But its no good saying to yourself '*Well that's OK then I don't need to worry about doing that until November*'. No, that's no good at all. What you have to do now is to divide the big project into twelve tasks which you can set yourself to complete by the end of each month. You could then divide each of these into four weekly tasks. By doing that you will ensure that the whole project is complete by the end of the year.

Stop wasting time

People find life entirely too time-consuming.   Stanislaw J. Lec

How do you spend your day? Do you know specifically? How long do you speak on the telephone, answer e-mails, drink coffee, talk to colleagues, watch television, and eat?

Action step

Keep a log of everything you do over 24 hours: jot down what you are doing every quarter of an hour and make a note every time you change activity.

Notice
- how long each phone call takes
- how much time you take having a cup of coffee
- how long you chat to a colleague about nothing in particular
- how much time you take for your lunch hour
- how much sitting and staring into space

- how long in the car or commuting on the tube or train or bus
- how long exercising

Keep a note of all your activities for a day or two.

What do you notice?

When are you are wasting time? What can you do differently to free up some time?

Dr B realises that he has long telephone conversations during the day. He decides to preface any future calls with 'I have five minutes available'. He keeps an eye on the clock and then at the end of that time concludes with: 'Sorry, but I have to go now.'

Dr. C takes much longer than the other doctors to see his patients. He lets them 'ramble on' and as he sorts out one thing for them they get into the 'while I'm here doctor'......scenario. He comes to terms with the 10 minutes he has allotted for each person and has a large clock on his desk so he can keep an eye on it. As the patient starts to talk about other things he learns techniques for getting them back on track. 'OK then, so is the bottom line that you have a new pain in your shoulder you are worried about....let's arrange to have it X-rayed and in the meantime take these tablets and see if they help.' He hands over the form and the prescription while standing up and going to the door.

How can **you** become more '**time aware**'?

Delegate

You have identified time wasters and are beginning to eliminate these. Now, look again at how you spend your day, notice what you are doing and if it is actually **your** job? Are you spending time doing tasks which **someone else** could or should be doing?

If you are a doctor and spend time filing patient notes ask if this is your job.

Even if you are short staffed, it is still not your job. You may believe you are helping a colleague but in fact you are masking a problem. If you are too busy would the clerical person do your clinic or surgery for you? Why not? Because it's not their job. You have very specialised skills and experience. Using them is what you are paid to do. So, make a list of tasks you do, and who **should** be doing them. Tell your colleagues that you will no longer be doing those things. Scary? Yes of course it is.

How come you are doing them?

Perhaps you offered to help out one day when things were busy and what started as a gesture of kindness has become an expectation.

It's often difficult to say 'no'

Saying 'no' more often, will have a huge impact on the time you have available to do what you want. What is the worst thing that can happen if you say no? What is the best thing that can happen if you say 'no'? If you say 'no' what are you saying 'yes' to?

How did it happen that you do someone else's work? Did you say yes for the sake of a quiet life? A quiet life for whom? A quiet external life maybe, but what about the turmoil and frustration you feel inside? Are you someone who agrees to do whatever you are asked? Do people say '*oh she'll do it*' or '*he'll do it*'?

Challenge your beliefs

What is it about saying **no** that you find difficult? What do you feel guilty about when you say no? Do you come up with a lot of '*shoulds*'? Complete the phrase: '*I should.......*' These will be some of your internal rules of life (your beliefs). How many 'shoulds' are on your list? Ask yourself after each statement '*Why?*' until you can't answer it any more.

Where do those beliefs come from? If they came from your parents, think about their situation, their childhood and how different it was from yours.

Remember that most parents do the best they can for their children. But they are influenced by what they learned from their parents and so on, ad infinitum. So their rules do not need to be your rules today. You are an adult now and can change the way you do things.

Now change the '*I should*' statements into '*I choose, (if I want)*' statements.

I should invite so and so over to dinner next week' to 'I choose, (if I want), to invite so and so for dinner next week and if you don't want them you can choose to say 'no' and not do it!

Make a list of your 'I choose (if I want)' statements, adapted form the 'I should' statements. How do you feel different when you read the 'I choose' compared with the 'I should'? It's about choice: you do have a choice, (you really do). You can choose the way you do this or do that: with a smile or with a frown.

What can you delegate to someone else?

- tasks you don't enjoy
- things which aren't your job to do
- routine tasks which you can train someone else to do

Dr C is increasingly frustrated by sorting through thick files whilst listening to her patients. She persuades her partners that the practice would benefit by employing a filing clerk who systematically tidies up the files.

In an effort to delegate tasks, Dr D does all the smears for the practice while Dr E sees all the patients with diabetes.

What can you not do?

What could you avoid or stop doing altogether? They may be things which do not need to be delegated because they **don't need to be done at all.**

When you've been through the 'why' questioning suggested, you may have identified some tasks which you have come to realise are on your 'to do' list because they are things which 'have always been done', rather than things which need to be done today in today's circumstances. Take them off your 'to do' list and you reduce your stress.

The GP who retired used to see pharmaceutical representatives whenever they chose to come into the Surgery. Even though they had to wait until he had seen some patients he always spent time with them. This irritated the new partner Dr F who didn't like the interruption. He decided to only see the Reps between 9 and 10 am on Wednesdays. Once they knew the changed routine the Reps co-operated and Dr F managed to leave the surgery on time regularly.

Stop procrastinating

Procrastination is the thief of time. Edward Young

Just get on and do the things you absolutely have to do. Why don't you? If you don't have the skills you need for the task, then acquire them. Find someone to help.

Dr G isn't very good with computers, so he asks his teenage son to help him.

Sometimes a task seems so big that its very size is off-putting. The approach is to break it down into bite sized chunks so that you make a start however small. For example: you need to clear the clutter of a lifetime and you realise this may take two weeks or more to complete. As you haven't got this to spare you end up not even starting because of time limitations. However if you recognise that even though you don't have two weeks or even a whole day to spend on the project, you do have an hour tomorrow morning.

So thinking of the big project what could you complete in an hour? Perhaps you could clear one quarter of your desk. So do it. And another quarter the next day and so on. You are getting it done. Chunk by chunk progress is being made!

Say no more often

Have you been asked to do something you don't really want to do? Sometimes it's difficult to say *'no'*. You may feel guilty, especially if someone is asking you for help. Saying *'no'* is a vital skill to develop if you want more time. Just say it, try not to get into a discussion about why. This is about you recognising your own needs and keeping within your personal boundaries. When you look at how you spend your day, if you find that a considerable amount of work is unplanned and consists of doing extras for others then saying 'no' is an important skill to acquire urgently.

When asked if he could 'just fill in this market research form,' Dr I replies he doesn't want to do that.

Asked if she would mind 'reading through this report and telling me what you think of it,' Dr J says she will do it later but not now.

Streamline your tasks

So you've freed up time, delegated things, got rid of others, decided not to procrastinate any more and learned how to say *'no'* However, there are still some tasks that have to be done by you. What else can you do?

Have you reached your *'enough is enough'* time?

Has your partner or spouse told you that things will have to change otherwise you can't stay together? Do you fear the break up of your partnership, your life, your world? Do you try to please all of the people all of the time and now realise that you are desperately unhappy and near to breaking point?

Go back through the suggestions in this chapter and decide on one thing you can change this week.

Devise systems for doing regular tasks

Having decided what you can delegate and what you can dump, are you as efficient as you can be in the tasks you have to do? Have you ever watched yourself and notice how streamlined you are in the way you do your tasks? How can you improve your systems?

Dr K realises that every time he wants to look up something in the British National Formulary he has to get out of his chair to reach it. He puts some bookends on his desk and keeps it within easy reach.

Dr L designates half an hour (timed) at the start and end of each day to read and answer emails.

Dr M decides the amount of time each day that she will use to sign prescriptions, the day of the month that she will check her credit card receipts, and the day and time each week when she will go to the gym.

What steps can you take this week to free up some time? Be specific about what you will do. Ask or tell the appropriate people about the changes you decide to make.

Who can support you?

Drs N, O, and P decide to support each other to make life better for them all. There is some resistance at first, but eventually their colleagues find the new way of running the practice works well and has the bonus of a much happier atmosphere between them.

Stephen Covey[26] suggests drawing a grid labelled:

1. **Urgent and Important e.g.** *medical crises; pressing problems; deadline driven projects; meetings; preparations*

26 Covey S, *First things first* Simon Schuster 1994

2. **Not urgent and Important** *e.g. preparation; prevention; values clarification; planning; relationship building; empowerment; true recreation*

3. **Urgent and Not Important** *e.g. interruptions; some phone-calls; some mail; some reports; some meetings*

4. **Not urgent and not Important** *e.g. trivia; busy work; junk mail; some phone calls; time wasters; 'escape' activities*

Many doctors spend their time doing things which are both *'urgent and important'*. However if you plan more carefully it's possible to do more in the *'important but not urgent'* segment; eliminate, by delegating, most of the *'urgent and not important'* tasks; and eliminate completely most of the *'non urgent /non important'* things (the time wasters)

So.....what will you do now?

Remember nothing changes until you take some action.

Chapter 8: No more procrastination

Procrastination is the art of keeping up with yesterday. Don Marquis

Excuses

You decide to change yet nothing happens because you don't actually put your ideas into practice. How come you are so good at delaying? What is it about you or your personality that means, in spite of all your good intentions, your ideas stay on the back burner? They simmer away, draining your energy and yet are never cooked enough to make a difference.

Is it because you are so busy each day that some things never get done, even when they reach the top of your 'to do' list? If so, perhaps you need to look at your time management skills. Do you regularly find a reason not to do what you promise? Are you angry when someone asks: '*Haven't you done that yet?*' because they don't understand how difficult life is for you. Some make excuses like:

There's no point in starting to clear the cupboard in my surgery desk as I haven't the time to finish it this afternoon.

I can't use the new software as I'm not sure how to apply it to my practice.

I don't have time to finish dictating letters because the patients talked too much.

Do you start each day putting aside tasks which have been in your head for days, weeks or months, because something more urgent has come to the top of your list? **When** will you actually do what you plan? The things which don't get done stay waiting, the thought of them lurking in the back of your mind, draining your energy.

What can you do?

You will have the jobs you've been putting off for ages done in record time. Sometimes when you are stuck in one task everything else is forgotten. Unfortunately there are always the urgent and important tasks which have to be dealt with under pressure. However if you've made an effort to put a routine in place for daily tasks which help you cope with it all then you will be able to get back on track again quickly.

- stop wasting time on non-urgent and non-important tasks
- plan your day more effectively
- write down what you want to do each day
- break the tasks into much smaller chunks
- get the file out
- develop efficient systems to be more efficient

Decide on a set of daily tasks and set yourself a time for each. Then move on to the next task even if you haven't finished the first one.

Change your routine

A very important part of time management is to stop things which **you** don't need to be doing. When thinking about getting things done consider whether what you are attempting to do is really on your own agenda or if it's because you are under pressure from someone else.

You may be doing things for no other reason except that *'it's the way it's always been done in this department'.* Is there another way to do it more efficiently or could some of the things be dropped as not being relevant any more?

Dr P knows he spends too much time on the internet or answering emails instead of getting more important tasks done. He sets a limit for emails and internet surfing to half an hour morning and evening.

What do you have to learn?

Do you need to acquire new skills to be more efficient? If you are you finding it difficult to keep up with information and ways of doing things, then admit this to yourself and tell your colleagues that you would like some assistance or support for some specific training instead of struggling to do it all.

Ways to learn

There are different ways you might do this.

- read journals and textbooks
- go on a course
- find support from others
- learn from the internet
- view an educational video or television programme
- discussion with colleagues
- 'hands on' approach of someone talking you through a procedure

Dr C, whose keyboard skills are not very good feels frustrated until he signs on for a course to learn to touch type and subsequently is less stressed.

Who can you ask?

It's OK to ask for assistance. You believe that you have to do it all and would appear incompetent if you ask for help. Talk about what you find stressful or difficult. Let go of your fear that others will see you as lacking ability if you admit that something is challenging. Ask yourself: *'What is the worst thing that could happen to me if I called for some support?'* You may be surprised at how ready people are to lend a hand when you ask and find they understand your difficulty. If they are not able or willing to assist you themselves they may suggest someone else who can. Wouldn't you do the same for them if they were struggling with something that was easy for you?

Just do it

You've delegated everything you can, you've surprised yourself and said 'no' more times than you thought possible without the world falling apart as a result, you've set up efficient systems and acquired all the skills you need to do the tasks without feeling incompetent. You've eliminated as much as possible after asking the question: *'Does this actually need to be done by me or indeed by anyone, or has it become a routine with no rationale?'* So there's no basis to procrastinate any longer. When will you take action? Make up your mind about what you are going to get done this week and *'just do it.'* No more excuses. If you are extremely clear about what you want to achieve then it is more likely you will succeed. Break huge tasks into *'bite sized pieces'* and make a start. **Don't wait any longer**.

Dr R wanted to get up to date with reading through the pile of medical journals but never got around to it. He decided to look through this week's BMJ for an hour on Friday afternoon and takes those older than one month, read or unread, for re-cycling.

What happens next?

You will get on with your life and do whatever you really want to do.

'Off days' are a part of life, I guess, whether you're a cartoonist, a neurosurgeon, or an air-traffic controller. Gary Larson

Know the true value of time; snatch, seize, and enjoy every moment of it. No idleness; no laziness; no procrastination; never put off till tomorrow what you can do today. Lord Chesterfield

Chapter 9: Looking after number one

Equipped for life

Your life in and out of medicine is full of gadgets and equipment all of which need regular servicing, maintenance and care. You may have been persuaded to take out a contract to cover every possibility. You are clear that disaster would strike if such and such didn't function the way it should, so you sign on the dotted line. You have covered yourself for all eventualities. This gives you some sort of satisfaction, since you know what you would miss most if it broke down and could no longer be mended.

What **is** the most vital piece of equipment for your medical practice? Is it your computer, your car or your mobile phone? How would you manage without one of them? Maybe you have some spares, or an older model kept in a cupboard, though it may need repairing, ready for any possibility. Perhaps colleagues would be willing to lend you theirs (for a while at least).

You live in a world dependent on technology working well and being available.

Dr. A has his computer operating system upgraded to the latest version. The newest practice management software is installed. Anti-virus software scans regularly. Everything should be working well but it isn't. One day he has to delay starting the surgery because the computer has crashed so he has no access to patient records or prescriptions.

Dr B is annoyed when the local garage tells him it will take three days to repair his car. He has to employ a driver at great expense to take him on his visits (and even more frustrating because most of them could have come to the surgery).

When Dr. C arrives at her out-patient clinic on the other side of the city she finds it has been cancelled because of shortage of nursing staff. No-one has been able to contact her as her mobile phone was switched off.

These examples remind you how much modern medical practice depends on equipment working well. How up to date are you? Is all your equipment serviced and upgraded regularly? Make a list of outstanding jobs you have in this area of your life.

What do you need to look after above all else? [27]

However careful you are, you may be neglecting the most important piece of technology in your life. **Yourself.** Do you fully take care of your most essential tool? Do you do the things that you know are good for your health and well being? Do you service yourself regularly and check that you work properly? Is your energy generated from the best source? Do you provide yourself with the most efficient fuel or do you poison yourself with alcohol, drugs, unhealthy food or nicotine?

Take a moment to think about yourself: your body, mind and spirit. Consider these as your own, your very own *'personal operating system,'* which needs as much or even more care and attention as all your other equipment put together. This **is** the most important machine you have and you know, better than most, that it cannot be replaced if and when it fails.

Does your system need optimising?

Are you functioning as well as you can? You may believe you are fighting fit and can do as much as you always could, yet somehow you don't feel the same as you did years ago and the sparkle isn't there as often. You want to get it back again but feel you have lost your enthusiasm for life.

You don't want your colleagues to see you as weak and unable to cope. Of course you don't. The culture still persists among the medical profession that doctors don't get ill and can cope with everything. Perhaps this is the reason you carry on bravely and tell people everything is fine, even though you know it isn't. You may be tempted to self-medicate or talk to a colleague about your 'friend' who has certain symptoms, instead of arranging a

27Clark S. Why do people become doctors and what can go wrong? *BMJ* 2000; 320: 2-3

professional consultation. Your colleagues probably know that you are not managing. They may talk about you behind your back and yet not give you the support you would like.

Pause for a moment. Take a look in the mirror. What you see? Does your face show the strain of the last few years?

Glance around at your colleagues. Are they happy at the thought of another day in the out-patient clinic, or are they fed up too? Are their faces tense and do they look tired? Of course it isn't right to make instant judgements about someone's appearance, however looking at yourself and the way you've changed over the years may be helpful.

In the course of your working week you advise many of your patients about ways to look after themselves better. You may tell them about giving up smoking, taking exercise and eating a healthy diet. **Do you walk your talk?** Do you follow the guidelines yourself or is it a case of *'do as I say not as I do'*?

Think about yourself

How can you make positive improvements in your life? Start with your diet. What can you do to improve this? How do you boost your energy when you are exhausted?

Are you poisoning yourself with excessive sugar, too much food, fats, caffeine, junk food, tobacco, alcohol or drugs, prescribed or otherwise? Can you think of other ways to feel more energetic, for example: taking a walk at lunch time, eating more fruit or vegetables?
Is your diet as nutritious and healthy as it could be?

When you look after yourself everything else works well and life becomes easier. The clinics may still have too many attending but you won't feel quite so stressed. The patients may be as demanding and rude but you will be able to cope much better.

Action step

Upgrade the way you look after yourself this week and notice how much better you feel.

Dr. B is too busy to eat anything at lunchtime and keeps herself going with cups of black coffee. She is exhausted at the end of the day. She decides to bring a sandwich and go over to the park to eat it quietly away from the hospital.

Mr C arrives on the ward out of breath. His only exercise is from the car to the clinic, clinic to ward, ward to car. He is putting on weight and has no energy. He decides enough is enough and it's time to do something for himself. He realises that it is only five miles to the hospital. He buys himself a new bike and uses the cycle route to and from work each day. He's surprised how quickly he gets there after the first week which is a bit of a struggle he gets used to the jokes from his colleagues and begins to feel more alert and energetic.

You'll do something when you're not so busy

Are you muttering under your breath as you read this? Are you thinking something along the lines of:

It's no good expecting me to make big changes when things are completely overwhelming. Yes, I know what to do and I'll do it one of these days. Just stop putting pressure on me to do it right now.

That's not good enough. If you want to change, that is not a valid excuse. Do you really believe that you'll wake up one day and say *'I'm not busy today.'* This is a delaying tactic. You can make a very small change today, if you decide to do so. Small changes grow into bigger changes. What very small change could you commit to making every day this week? If you really want things to improve you have to find the time you need. How much time does it take to choose a healthy dessert instead of a pudding, or have a piece of fruit instead of a bar of chocolate? Of course you can do it even if you are busy. The only thing that stops you is your own mental attitude. Change from saying to yourself: *'I don't have time'* to *'I have all the time I need to make a small change today.'* Do it now before it's too late.

When your BMJ arrives do you go to the Obituaries first? Does that make you aware of your own mortality? Now is the time to take stock, to change things, step by small step, even while you are busy. Suppose you realise you don't eat enough fruit each day. To eat five portions may seem impossible so how about starting with one piece? Instead of dismissing the big change as not possible, do a bite sized version of it. Commit yourself to introducing your new habit, however small that may be, on a daily basis from today.

Imagine your working day as enjoyable, stress free and with everything going smoothly and   at last you have the time to start looking after yourself more. What would you do? How could you improve yourself? Would you start with your mind, your body or your spirit? Just one new habit this week. Make the commitment. It's often motivating to have someone to be answerable to. Is there a friend or colleague who could encourage and inspire you to keep going for the first few days when it may seem an impossible prospect to change the routine of many years?

Drs X and Y who live near each other and not too far from the surgery decide to meet at the end of the road and walk together to and from work.

Drs P and Q realise how unhealthy their diet is and so they decide to take it in turns to bring a healthy packed lunch.

It's time to listen to yourself and take the advice you already know and regularly give to your patients. These headings serve as reminders.

For a healthy body

Which of these can you do?

- eat a balanced diet, if you are overweight this includes eating less

- reduce the amount of caffeine, sugar and fat in your diet
- eat plenty of fresh fruit and vegetables
- don't smoke
- exercise regularly: walking is as good as anything
- stretch with Yoga or Pilates
- aerobic exercise: running; dancing; cycling
- drink alcohol in moderation
- avoid unnecessary medication
- seek advice rather than self prescribe

For a healthy mind

- be curious
- ask questions
- take chances
- recognise your needs and satisfy them.
- don't expect your nearest and dearest to be all things to you
- learn new things
- be dedicated to lifelong learning (and not just medicine!)
- be open to possibilities
- get out of your rut and follow wherever your spirit leads you

For a healthy spirit[28]

- take time for yourself: meditate or sit quietly away from others; spend time in nature; by water or whatever puts your inner self at peace for a few minutes each day
- spend time with your family. Maintain your priorities: if you have small children, they only take their first step once
- be involved in your community
- do what you are passionate about: a feeling of joy and well-being comes from doing something you really love to do
- be at peace: let go of anger, frustration and fear

28 Paul Elliston Mindfulness in medicine and everyday life *BMJ* 2001;323:S2-7322

Whatever is happening is what is perfect for you at this time. Find the positive amongst the negative and relax. However much people irritate or anger you, be more accepting. Whatever will be is for the best. It's time to let go of your wish to be in control and trust that others will do whatever needs to be done.

You can do it. Start, step by step. Introduce the changes you want to make one by one, week by week. Some people find it helps to make a list of *'daily habits'*. These could start with one or two small things you can easily introduce into your routine. Week by week add another new habit. Do these regularly each week until after about a month they become automatic.

Go on, give yourself the greatest chance to live the best life you possibly can. Don't make any more excuses. Start today with one or two small changes. It won't take long for you to understand how much better your life can be.

Five ways to survive as a doctor [29]

- make sure you do things other than work
- create your dream work schedule
- learn to say no, without feeling guilty
- if you need help, ask for it
- seek peer support

---

29 Berger A. Surviving (and even enjoying) medicine BMJ 2000; 320

Chapter 10: What's draining you?

Here you are

You wonder if anything can ever change. You resign yourself to feeling like you do for the rest of your life, even though that makes you feel very unhappy. What else can you possibly do? You've done all the things the personal development books tell you to do. You've perfected your time management skills, looked after your mind, body and spirit until they are all shining beacons to anyone who wants to look and yet you still feel drained at the end of the day. You wonder if things will ever be better and if you can be *'full of the joys of spring'* again. Or even the joys of autumn.

As you sit down at your untidy desk you dread the thought of putting it in order. The task would take days to complete and there never seems to be a spare moment, let alone a spare day to do that. You shy away from throwing out your piles of old medical journals until you've sat down and read them all, or at least skimmed through them. You might throw away an important article.

Clear the clutter

The *'clutter-clearing'* malarkey is something you've studiously avoided. Perhaps you've read about how clearing out your unwanted junk can be useful to clear a space for other things to happen. But you're always too tired to start doing any of that. Have you been amazed at those television programme participants who allow someone to clear everything out of their house and then put up with the ritual humiliation of having all their possessions scrutinised on air?

Maybe you've wondered how can a few tidy drawers help to find the right job? How indeed? There's something going on, no-one understands what it is, but it works. Some call it synchronicity or serendipity, others call it good luck or fate or random chance. But whatever it is, it happens. Whether you like it or not, changing one thing in your life enables other things to happen. No doubt like most of us, you have cupboards and drawers full of old clothes and shoes which you know you will never wear again, or that you'll be slim enough to fit into once more. Dream on!

Life is like a spreadsheet, alter one element and everything else automatically adjusts. Be more aware and notice what happens, what starts to come into your life when you create the space. Try clearing a few drawers and watch out for the opportunities which come your way. Hocus pocus? Or metaphysics? Do we have to know how or why something occurs?
If you really want to attract things into your life to be happy and more content, here is the simple formula:

GET RID OF WHAT DRAINS YOU
DO MORE OF WHAT ENERGISES YOU

Your environment

Home

Is it the way you want it? Have you unpacked all the boxes in the attic? Is the furniture what you love: or is it what friends and family off loaded on to you? The lighting: is it in the right place for what you want to do? The temperature: are you too hot or too cold? How about the colour scheme: does it make your heart sing? Is there too much clutter lying around? How much more can you tolerate? How much time can you commit to clearing some papers each day? What do you need to do to stop more mess accumulating?

Geographical

Do you live and work where you want to be? If not, have you thought about your ideal environment? The first step to making any change is imagining what it is that you want. Once you can see it in your mind's eye then it will begin to happen. Involve all your senses. Is your current situation too noisy or too quiet, too urban or too rural? Thinking about where you are and where you want to be, is a small step you can make **now**.

Dr. D wants to live by the sea so in the meantime makes sure he goes there at least once a month.

Your relationships

Work

Do you get on well with your colleagues? Do you communicate with them regularly and talk and listen to each other? If you want something at work can you explain, listen and be heard and be prepared to try other options.

Personal

Do you have a happy close relationship? Do you listen and talk? Do you seek to understand and then be understood?[30] Do you have friends who nurture rather than drain you?

Community

Are you part of a supportive community of people who share your interests? Do you give and receive support from those who are part of it?

You, the person

Who are you without the professional label? Your needs: what are they and are they being met? Your values: are you living by yours[31]?

Your body

Look after yourself[32]

30 Covey, S *The seven habits of highly effective people.* 1989.
31 Houghton A. Values? What values? BMJ 2002;324:S59
32 Kersley S. Looking after number one. BMJ 2002;324:S85

Money

Are you earning enough? Are you saving for the future? Are you wasting money? Can you afford your lifestyle?

Make a list

Note everything you can think of which is draining you. Start with ten things. Expand each by making them very specific. If you have written a person's name establish what specifically about that person that annoys you (and use the opportunity to reflect whether what really annoys you about others is actually something in you). Keep adding to your list until you have at least a hundred things on it. Then get rid of everything on the list.

Start with the easy things

For example you could:

- throw away the broken printer that you know will never get mended
- take all your old medical journals to be recycled
- buy the extra gadget or pair of scissors or screwdriver, so you don't have to spend time looking where you last put it down
- go through your credit card receipts or bank statements regularly
- repair the dripping tap or call a plumber to do it
- pay someone to do the housework
- clear your clutter bit by bit, piece by piece

Let your heart sing

What would do it for you? Could it be:

- a place you love to go
- music you adore
- friends you haven't seen for ages

- being alone in nature
- special people
- walking in the countryside

Whatever is your passion, bring it back into your life. You've made excuses long enough. Make time for whatever energises you. Even an hour a week is enough to get you off the treadmill of life to recharge your batteries. Find a time to be creative, to be in touch again with who you are and to gain a new perspective on your life.

The outcome will be:

- space for everything
- more energy
- more fun

Don't wait any longer

Chapter 11: Living an abundant life

Imagine what it would be like to have a cup of life so full it runs over with contentment, confidence and satisfaction.

Is your life half empty or half full? Are you stuck in *'scarcity mode'*? Do you avoid making changes in case the barrel of life has no more to offer? Are you nervous about *'letting go'* in case you never get a refill? Or are you confident there will always be more than enough to go round and closing one door allows others to open?

What does it mean to live abundantly?

The important parts of your life can be represented on a *'life's wheel.'*[33] This is a pie chart divided into equal segments, each representing an area of life that is important for a fulfilled and balanced life.[34]

How much of your life has too low a score? Which one takes too much of your energy from the others? What can you do in a part of your life that you neglect?

It is possible to shift from a negative view of the world to a more positive attitude. If you can do this does it mean that your 'glass' is not only full but overflows and it is possible to have more than you could possibly need?

Are you ready for the challenge?

Start by picturing your ideal circumstances. Imagine someone looking at you living that life. What would they see?

Time

Is finding more time a priority? What can you stop doing to free up time to

33 Cameron J. *The artist's way.* London: Pan books, 1995:57.
34 Kersley, S. Striking the balance *BMJ* 2001; 323 S2

do something you love? What will you say 'no' to? Do you recognise the bonus of extra time if a meeting or trip is cancelled?

Dr A is disappointed when she fails to get the consultant job she wants. She decides to use the time to travel for a few months instead.

Dr B is ambivalent about whether or not to attend a conference in her own time. She realises that instead of jet lag and exhausting flights she could tidy her office and paint some pictures in the time available.

Money

Money is better than poverty, if only for financial reasons.   Woody Allen

Is more money the answer? It certainly helps. Do you need to make external or internal changes around money? If you never have enough is this a result of spending beyond your means or buying unnecessarily? Do you make your money work for you or do you work for your money?

The state of your financial health may derive from your family and their way of life. Are their beliefs relevant to you and your life today? If they feed your feeling of never having enough, how can you change these beliefs? How about making a subtle shift and putting yourself first for a change; each month decide how much is for you to save and to spend. Look at what's left and decide which expenses to reduce.[35]

Money is like a sixth sense without which you cannot make a complete use of the other five. W Somerset Maugham

Stock up on everything

Start with something easy and useful: for example, household goods (and I'm not joking). Even something as simple as knowing you don't have to

---

35 Kiyosaki RT   *Rich dad poor dad.* London: Warner books, 2002.

buy these items for ages can begin to ease the pressure of thinking about mundane tasks and give you the sense of abundance[36]

What else do you have to keep on replacing? Would having more of whatever it is relieve some of the drain on your energy? You see, abundance is about having plenty of energy, space, light, health, and friends, as well as time and money. You can work towards having enough of everything. Maybe you need to look at what is 'enough.' Are there adjustments you can make to your lifestyle to allow you to have more of the life you really want? Thinking about what motivates you may help with this.

Give something away

What can you be generous with apart from money? What can you give away: time, love, expertise or friendship? What else? Some people say that what you give returns to you eventually, in some way or another. So by giving, your reserves will grow.

I'd rather have roses on my table than diamonds on my neck.
Emma Goldman

What else?

An abundant life means having more than you need in every aspect of your life. It doesn't depend on the amount of money in the bank. It relies on building resources of everything when you can, so that in lean times you will have stores not only of money but also of time, love, learning, ideas, and fun. If you do, you will have the following to look forward to:
- a fulfilled life in and out of medical practice
- money to live the life you want
- time for friends, family, yourself, and your community
- love
- learning
- fun and laughter

36 Leonard TJ *The portable coach.* New York: Scribner, 1998:53.

Chapter 12: Relationship: what relationship?

Is there something about close personal relationships that is particularly difficult for doctors? If you and your partner are both medics, you share an understanding of the reality of working in the medical profession. Does your similar background lead to frustration and resentment if one of you is more successful than the other?

Connections

Did you meet when you were both students, two like minded people in potentially an ideal partnership? Were you both working in the same speciality and that sparked your interest in each other?

Do you sometimes wonder whether it would have been better to have partnered instead with someone as far removed from the medical world as possible?

Coping

How do you cope with on-call responsibilities especially when you have young children?

Dr A, a GP, and her husband Mr B a surgeon, paid for a babysitter even though one or other of them was usually in the house, in case they were both called out at the same time.

Dr. C, another GP, arranged to be on call on different days from her husband, Dr D an anaesthetist, so that one of them could look after the children. This resulted in them never having time together, free from the persistent phone.

Compromise

Is your social life non-existent because one of you has an emergency to deal with at the time you were supposed to be going out? Do you come home too tired to do anything?

Do you find yourself wondering what happened to the person you fell for when you were both students or worked in the same hospital as junior doctors? Do you wonder whether he or she fancies the night sister or charge nurse more than you?

Do you both expect everything to be organised around you? Do you wish you had a support team so that life at home would be as straightforward as going into theatre to do an operation? Are you so used to telling others what to do and having your requests carried out that you find it exasperating when he or she refuses to do something? Do you bring home the tension of the day? And regret how quickly you lose your temper? Have many of your friends in similar situations separated or divorced? Is your relationship doomed too?

Considerations

Bear in mind that home is different from work. Doctors are used to telling people what to do but don't like others telling them. As a doctor you have excellent communication skills. Do you use them to communicate with your partner? Are you too busy looking after others to take time for your relationship?

Co-operation

You have both moved on, your career aspirations may not be the same as they were years ago. Perhaps you have children now and one of you wants to put their career on hold in order to look after them.

Is it time to make some changes in the way you live? When was the last time you tried to understand what life is like for him or her?

What is the most important thing for you? Is it progressing in your career or being with your partner and children? Or have you been delaying starting a family until you reach a certain stage? Are you worrying that you are getting older and know it's time to make decisions?

Whatever happened in the past has contributed and enriched your life one way or another. There is always something positive to learn from every experience however negative it seems at the time. If you've been unlucky in your close relationships, please take a moment to consider what you learned to help you do better next time. What worked and what didn't work?

Communication

Do you listen twice as much as talk to your partner? Remember when you last had a fun time together. Successful relationships depend on a number of things:

- being clear about boundaries
- letting go of trying to control someone else
- respecting your needs may be different from theirs
- realising that you are a worthwhile person in your own right - your partner is too
- finding areas of common interest
- doing what you love to do and let your partner do whatever gives him or her joy
- saying no this week to things you no longer want to do
- taking time to do something with your partner that you both enjoy

Dr X realised that he and his wife Dr Y only ever spoke about domestic matters. He remembered how much they used to enjoy walking in the countryside near their home. He made a decision to ask her to have a long walk with him at the weekend. She was very pleased to do that and it was an opportunity to talk again.

Take time also to do something you really enjoy **without** your partner. Remember what it felt like before you were a 'doctor's partner' and try to recapture that feeling again. Go on, indulge yourself!
Don't make any more excuses about why you can't do this. Make a start today with something, however small.

Chapter 13: Ten top tips for achieving your goals

1. Make your goal SPECIFIC

Are your goals too vague? Some amazing goals aren't achievable because they are too vague. If you have a goal, for example *'I want to be happier'* then ask yourself *'happier than what?'* What does being happier mean to you? What will you be doing when you are happier? How will you recognise yourself as happier? It's a great goal but not specific enough. If you connect being happier with let's say spending time with your family, then a specific goal from this might be *'I want to spend an afternoon each week with my family'.*
If you are happy when you go to the cinema then you might say to yourself: *'My goal is to go to the cinema once each week'.*

2. Your goal should be MEASURABLE

How will you know when you've achieved your goal? This follows from making your goal specific. If you decide to get a new job, then you either have or haven't got a new job. It's *'measurable.'* If you decide to run in a marathon next year, then you will know when you've done it. If however you decide to be happier it's more difficult to measure *'happier'* or to know if you've achieved it.

3. Make sure your goal is ACHIEVABLE

Is your goal something that you are capable of doing? For example if you are overweight and unfit and eighty years old and you decide your goal is to win a gold medal for running at the next Olympics then perhaps that is not an achievable goal.

4. Is your goal REALISTIC

If you are a lightweight woman and your goal is to lift a bus on to your shoulders then your goal is not realistic.

5. By WHEN do you want to achieve the goal?

It is very important for your goal to be timed. You may decide that by the end of the year you want to lose a certain amount of weight. So decide a date when you will achieve this.

6. WRITE your goals

There is a story about a group of college students who where asked, when they graduated, to write down what they wanted to achieve in their lives. It is said that when they were contacted some years later those that had clear goals were more likely to have achieved them. Whether this is true or not, keeping a written record of your goals gives you something to refer to in the future and a way to assess how your life is going and whether you still want the same as you did years ago. It's OK to make changes as you grow and your life evolves!

7. DECIDE the first steps

Work out what you want to achieve in the next six months, the next three months, the next month, the next week in order to get to the goal in, for example, a years time.

8. Keep a JOURNAL

Write something each day. Write your thoughts and feelings. Just let your hand move across the page (flow of consciousness writing). Don't censor what you write and don't re-read it immediately or correct it. As time goes by you will learn how this process frees up your mind to be much more creative and you may find that you have ideas about how to progress or how to move out of a stuck situation.

9. DO SOMETHING, however small, each day

The way to get things done is to make a start and take action. Even five or ten minutes a day contributes to the whole and is a better technique than waiting for some never to arrive day when you might have plenty of time.

10. CELEBRATE

If you follow these tips, you **will** achieve your goals. Tell yourself how well you've done and do something special to celebrate your success.

YOU CAN DO IT!!

PART THREE
Medicine is more than a job: it's a lifestyle

When making a decision of minor importance, I have always found it advantageous to consider all the pros and cons. In vital matters, however, such as the choice of a mate or a profession, the decision should come from the unconscious, from somewhere within ourselves. In the important decisions of personal life, we should be governed, I think, by the deep inner needs of our nature. Sigmund Freud

The tragedy of life is not that it ends so soon, but that we wait so long to begin it. W. M. Lewis

Chapter 14: Who heals the healers?

Expectations

Being a doctor may be a difficult role since there are all sorts of expectations placed on you. These go beyond your working day and may permeate your very being. Wherever and whenever someone knows you are medically qualified, you are expected to be able to deal with an emergency anywhere, anytime, any place. You have to know the answer about what to do and not show any weakness. Your colleagues, or so you strongly believe, know it all and you don't want to be shown up when you are amongst them. So it goes on. Some of this is a perpetuating myth. Of course, as a doctor, you **are** vulnerable, you **do** get upset, there are times when you don't know what to do and times when you feel emotional or unable to cope. Who can **you** turn to? Who can **you** share your emotions with? Very often the answer is no-one and so these feelings are ignored for a long time.

Support

Who do you turn to when you begin to wonder how you'll get through the next few years, or even the next few hours or days? Ideally the answer is someone in whom you can confide who will listen to you without judgement and accepts you as you are, with only your agenda. Do you believe that if you ask for help and support that this will be seen as your Achilles' heel? Do you, like some doctors, build a sort of outer protective skin around your emotional self, so that it's impossible or very difficult for people to make contact or connections with you? Are you vulnerable and frightened about seeking help for yourself because you think you have to cope on your own? Do you not want to admit that you don't know all the answers? Do you believe that others will think less of you if you admit ignorance? To avoid this:

- avoid putting obstacles between you and other people
- don't put up barriers to communication
- avoid jumping to conclusions

If you gave your absolutely full attention, truly listening to what the person is saying, then it is more likely that they will do it for you too. Have you ever experienced another person really hearing you? What we give out we get back and if you want someone to hear you then it's important to be a much, much better listener to others.

Find someone who you would feel comfortable to talk to and make a request of them. Tell them that you want them to truly listen to what you say.

Ask them not to tell you what to do, only reflect back to you to indicate that they have really heard you.

If you've got into the habit of jumping to conclusions when someone starts to tell you something, it may be valuable for you to find a basic counselling course to improve your listening skills and also experience the power of being truly listened to, yourself.

As an alternative, ask someone to be a listening partner, in order to give and experience this. No comments, no advice, just unadulterated listening for a set time each, with feedback at the end (*'what I hear is ......'*) This technique is used in co-counselling. Are you going to wait until you are at crisis point? Who can support you now? Who can be there for you and accept you and who you are[37]?

Without more ado

Now is the right time to improve the quality of your life so that you have time for family as well as patients. More opportunities to enjoy being away from work doing stuff you haven't done for years like going for a walk, a cycle ride, reading a book, painting, writing, any other almost forgotten hobby, whatever you've been saying to yourself, *'one day I'll have time for such'*. Now is the time to get more balance between your medical work and the rest of your life connecting with the part of you denied for years.

Don't wait until you're well and truly *'burnt out'*. Re-discover who you are.

---

37 Miller, L. The doctors support line. BMJ 2002;325:S117

Start today to make small changes. Be clear about what you have to do against what you *'should'* do.
Teach others your skills so that you can delegate the rest.

Self-care

You may believe that you are indispensable, but if you become too ill to work, what then? Be more *'selfish.'* The word *'selfish'* may have bad connotations for you. Think about it meaning *'self-care.'* If you take more care of yourself and your own needs you will cope much more effortlessly with those of your patients. Don't wait to find solace in drink, drugs or until you reach crisis point. Find someone to encourage and support you unconditionally. Talk to about your frustrations and difficulties of overwork in an environment of feeling undervalued and endless demands made of you.

Supervision

Counsellors are always supported by regular supervision from someone to help them to sort out what issues are the client's and what is their own stuff. Once you experience this support, it is difficult to know how you managed before. It is not to do with your standard of practice but about having someone to offload on to, without fear of recrimination, from a person with whom you don't have to keep up the front of perfection. Some doctors are beginning to recognise its value.[38] Perhaps it would be more acceptable for doctors if it had a different name.

When you experience the power of support and encouragement rather than demands and intimidation you will be more able to coach your patients to do whatever they need to do, rather than reaching for the prescription pad or becoming exasperated with them. When someone listens to your concerns and acknowledges them as legitimate, you will become a better listener to your patients and hear more of their underlying issues and empower them too. You will be able to convey to them that they can make a difference to

38 Wilson, Hamish J. Self-care for GPs; the role of supervision. New Zealand Family Physician 2000;27(5):51-57

their own lives when they take responsibility for it. Every small change you as an individual make will eventually help to change the system. Take courage: start to care for yourself, much more. What will you do differently today?

We deceive ourselves when we fancy that only weakness needs support. Strength needs it far more. Madame Swetchine

Chapter 15: Well-being - reality or dream?

The best six doctors anywhere
And no one can deny it
Are sunshine, water, rest, and air
Exercise and diet.
These six will gladly you attend
If only you are willing
Your mind they'll ease
Your will they'll mend
And charge you not a shilling.
Nursery rhyme quoted by Wayne Fields

It's easy to become so engulfed in work issues that you are too tired to enjoy yourself away from the hospital or your Practice.

Well-being

A state of '*being well, healthy, contented etc*'[39] '*the state of feeling healthy and happy*'.[40]
It's about the connection between your mind, body and spirit.[41] [42]

Is this how you are? Or is it a dim and distant memory of how you used to be? Do you look back with longing to a time when you really enjoyed seeing your patients and greeted each day with excitement? What's changed? How can you get the sparkle back?

Imagine a wooden beam steady on a narrow fulcrum. It moves to one side and then to the other. Over all, however, it maintains its equilibrium. I'd like to invite you to think of this balance as a metaphor. At one end is you and your life, at the other the patient and theirs.

39 *Oxford English Reference Dictionary,* Oxford University Press 1996
40 *Cambridge International Dictionary of English;* Cambridge University Press 2002
41 Chopra, Deepak *Quantum Healing,* Bantam Books, 1989
42 Siegel, Bernie, *Love Medicine and Miracles,* Harper Perennial,1986

As you deal with each patient, even though you try to keep the sense of balance fairly steady, sometimes you tip too far over on the patient's side and you feel tired and drained. Other times, you move more to your side and you are energised, happy and satisfied with the outcome of your work. If, day after day, week after week you find that you are giving out far more than you get back and the balance of your life is almost perpetually tilted away from your own needs and values, then perhaps it's time to redress the situation.

What can tip the balance one way or the other? How can you maintain more equilibrium in your life? What can you do to get back or maintain the well-being, the quality of life you so want?

Put yourself first

Being selfish is not always considered to be an enviable trait. But why not? Surely your own needs are of paramount importance? It's OK to look after yourself, physically, mentally and spiritually. If you take more care of yourself and your own needs you will cope more effortlessly with the needs of your patients. Don't wait until you find solace in drink or drugs. Don't wait until you reach crisis point. Start now. Find someone to encourage and support you unconditionally to achieve whatever you want. Who can you talk to about your frustrations of overwork as a doctor who feels undervalued and finding it difficult to cope with endless demands of the system? Do you have a mentor, partner or close friend who will listen to your concerns and acknowledge them as legitimate?

Take a break

When was the last time you felt uplifted? Moved? Energised? Quite simply, when did you take some time out for yourself? Do you know that even five or ten minutes each day just for you can make a profound difference?

Dr A. walks out of the hospital door each day at lunchtime and goes to a nearby park to eat his sandwiches and breathe some fresh air.

Dr. B packs her swimming things in her car and goes home via the swimming pool. After swimming a number of lengths she feels ready to deal with her domestic commitments and family.

Dr. C walks her dog each evening for half an hour.

Dr. D meditates regularly.

When did you last have a holiday? How about being a tourist for a day and visit somewhere locally? Is your life in tune with your values[43]? Are you nourishing your body, mind and spirit?

Big changes start with very small steps

Do you hear yourself saying *'One day I'll have time for such and such'*. What are you waiting for? Without doubt **NOW** is the time to get some more balance between your medical work and the rest of your life. Surely, **now** is the moment to begin to improve the quality of your life so that you can have time for family as well as patients, for your friends as well as your colleagues, for your community as well as for yourself? You could enjoy again doing things you haven't done for years.

Re-discover who you are

Don't wait until you're *'burnt out'*. Be clear what you have to do against what you *'should'* do. Teach others your skills so that you can delegate more. Do you think that you are indispensable and no-one else can do what you do?

Have you ever had to take time away from work and noticed that somehow or other they have managed without you?

Life has its ebbs and floes

Even if you are the most positive person you may have some days when you

43 Houghton, A Values? What values? BMJ 2002; 324: S59

are a bit down. Try to remember that without the off days you may not appreciate so much the good times. Who can you talk to?[44]

Body, mind and spirit are interconnected

If you are lacking in one area and don't know how to improve things, concentrate on nurturing another of them. Notice how when you do that, other parts of your life improve too.[45]

Keep a journal

Are you in the midst of a major transition at work or at home? It's easy to believe that things can't improve. Some people find it useful to track their moods and become aware of circumstances or situations which make them better or worse. You may find the process brings the insight you seek.

Become more aware

Laughter is said to be the best medicine. What makes you happy and feel on top of the world? Notice what you are doing when you feel great. Keep a *'treasure store'* of things to do for days when you feel that things could be better. This could include, for example, ideas about places to visit, people to call, music to listen to, something to create, exercises to do, inspiring books to read or tapes to listen to; something delicious to eat. What would be on your list?

Develop a positive mental attitude

This is probably the most important shift you can make to improve the way you are and your feeling of well-being. Your attitude affects the way you are and that affects the way others are towards you.

Dr D feels annoyed about some of the practice staff who seem unfriendly. He hasn't realised that they are reacting to his scowls, until he greets them

44 Miller, L The doctors support line *BMJ* 2002;325:S117
45 Yamey, G, Wilkes M, Promoting wellbeing among doctors. BMJ2001; 322:252-3

with 'Good morning, how are you today?' with a big smile. To his amazement they suddenly become friendly and quite human!

What we give out we give back. If you are unhappy in a situation think about what signals are coming from your verbal or body language, reflected in the way that person reacts to you. Become more aware of the words you use. Do you tend to moan about how awful things are? Do you use words like battle or struggle? You can change the way you regard a situation.

Live in the present

Enjoy whatever is happening in your life now. What are you learning? What will you do differently next time? What can you do to improve things? Who do you need to have a conversation with? Who can you encourage and validate today? Here's a challenge for you. Think of someone who you don't like or who irritates you and tell them something you admire about them.

Nurture your supportive networks

Have you considered being part of a support group? Be there for others and they will be there for you when you need them. Share and celebrate your good times.

Take regular time out

Arrange outings, holidays, time away from work. Reading is good too, so make time for books apart from medical textbooks and journals. Refresh you body, mind and spirit and notice the effect on your whole life.

Remind yourself of things going well

Keep thank-you letters from grateful patients. This is a wonderful morale booster to read if you feel low.

Create the future you want

To do this successfully it helps if you can:

- picture it in your mind
- feel, hear and smell it
- believe in yourself
- repeat positive affirmations each day as though what you want is already happening for example *'I am happy and content in my work and at home'*

What is a doctor to do?

Here is a summary of an informal survey I conducted amongst a few doctors.[46]

To maintain well-being, the surveyed doctors:

See friends and family; sleep; exercise; play music and sing; pray; take a holiday; eat; cook; walk the dog; go to the cinema; photography; laugh; swim; scuba dive; go to the gym; have a hot bath; take vitamins and other dietary supplements; designate time for self; count blessings; maintain a life outside of medicine; have glass of red wine; enjoy their partner and children; practice yoga; take a holiday.

To maintain well being of their body, they:

Walk to work; walk the dog; do aqua-aerobics; have enough sleep and rest; eat a decent diet; exercise regularly; play tennis; wear nice clothes; do yoga; cycle; swim; steam room; sauna and Jacuzzi; martial arts; running.

To maintain the well being of their mind, the doctors replied that they:

Have a range of interests; get a balance between work and life; are spiritual;

46 *Doctors talking* January 2003 www.thedoctorscoach.co.uk/doctorstalking.htm

play; maintain family life; get plenty of sleep; good food; exercise and have fun; keep a sense of humour; look at the BIG picture of life; read; spend time praying; write morning pages; practise their hobbies; drink wine; cook; attend courses; travel; remember the good times; laugh, spend time with friends; listen to music; go to the theatre; paint; sculpt; seek creative challenges; have fun and acquire new knowledge.

For the well-being of their spirit they:

Spend time with friends and family; take holidays, look at art; attend mass; meditate; sing in church choir; pray; go to church; count their blessings; be in the moment; watch the sun, sky, sea; read inspiring books; read poetry; be involved in freemasonry; listen to classical music; look after personal relationships; visit a temple; yoga.

How about you?

How do you, or will you, maintain your well-being now?

The patient's treatment begins with the doctor, so to speak. Only if the doctor knows how to cope with himself and his own problems will he be able to teach the patient to do the same. C. G. Jung

Chapter 16: Do your colleagues understand?

Communication is a skill that you can learn. It's like riding a bicycle or typing. If you're willing to work at it, you can rapidly improve the quality of every part of your life.
Brian Tracy

Good communication is as stimulating as black coffee and just as hard to sleep after.
Anne Morrow Lindbergh

Do you say what you really mean to say, or are you inhibited because you are sure they will think this or the other? So instead, you wait silently wishing you had the courage to speak up, to say what is in your head. Maybe you wish you knew more, scared to admit gaps in your knowledge and that you don't know everything there is to know about the subject. Your mind may be racing, desperately searching for the right words which you think are required. Then you realise that the moment has passed, again. You are silent, so at least no-one could hear how little you know. Are you as stupid as you believe? In the past perhaps you said something and your senior thought the way to respond was to ridicule you in front of your colleagues and the patient. Is this a good culture for learning? It is more helpful if your answer is acknowledged and accepted. You have studied for years and you are expressing what you know. There may be more. There may be extra examples you could have given. So, instead of humiliating you, your questioner could have thanked you for your answer and asked '*what else is there?*' or added *'there are a few other things you might want to mention next time…..'* Finally you could be thanked again for your contribution.

As a medical student I was the sole female on my medical firm (at that time there was a quota of 10% for female students!). I have a vivid memory of the consultant who rarely looked at or acknowledged me unless it was to put me down with his endless questioning and no acknowledgment of any correct answers given

Communication is a very important skill

You probably believe you are pretty good at communicating. After all you spend a lot of your time with patients, don't you? But do you really connect with them or as you hear certain clues, or certain symptoms, is your finger poised over the modern equivalent of the prescription pad, the computer key, ready to print out the appropriate treatment? In a busy surgery or clinic this can be entirely appropriate, the way you've adapted to the limited time available to see the maximum number of patients, but communication is about more than that, isn't it? It's about inter-action, an exchange of ideas, a two way process of listening and talking. Improving your communication skills can benefit the way you relate with both medical colleagues and other health professionals. Good communication is about recognising that they have something valuable to say as well. You learn from them as much as they do from you. It's about realising that you don't know everything and the other person may have something useful to contribute.

Think about it. How well **do** you get on with others at work? Are you irritated by people who either never say much or who don't co-operate? Have you ever considered it may be because they feel their input is unimportant or not worth much. Is this because of the way you've spoken to them and dismissed what they say, or made a judgement based on scanty evidence that they wouldn't have anything to contribute to a discussion about so and so. If you are annoyed by something about them, you could try congratulating them on something they do correctly before launching into an attack about what you consider is incorrect. You don't like to be told that everything you do is wrong. By hearing that something is correct and being told '*well done*', you are more receptive to the learning you need to do.

How could you improve your on-going communication with your practice partners, fellow consultants, registrars or colleagues you work with regularly? Start by thinking about the different opportunities there are for exchanging information. You probably have one or more of the following for regular contact with colleagues:

Formal departmental meetings

Are you the leader or a participant? If the chairperson, do you allow time for everyone present to have their say? Do you notice if someone is dominating the meeting and, if so, ask them to wait for a moment to let some of the quieter people present have their say too? When someone contributes, do you always thank them for their input or are you too quick to tell them that their idea couldn't work or is wrong? Have you a clear agenda and been specific about the length of the meeting, its purpose and the expected outcome? Or do you tend to ramble on for ages with people closing their eyes, or leaving because they thought the meeting would be shorter and they have other commitments?

If you are a participant, do you find meetings useful or are they long and boring? Do you feel you had the opportunity to have your say or is it dominated by one or two outspoken members? Are you always clear about the intended purpose and outcome for the meeting? If not, do you give constructive feedback to the chairperson?

Informal meetings

You may find these are easier in which to have your say. Perhaps you chat with colleagues over a quick lunch to sort something out. There are likely to be constant interruptions by mobile phones and others coming to your table with *'can I have a quick word with you about so and so?'* It's not an ideal situation is it? These circumstances are not best if you want to discuss any deeper issues. Instead of casual, chance meetings with the person you want to talk to, make an arrangement to talk at a definite time. *'Can I speak to you for about twenty minutes later today? When would be best for you?'*

Notice boards

Do you read them? Do others? Are they so crowded with old notices so that no-one sees the flyer you put up for a meeting, or about the information you want? Does someone take away out of date notices? How can you make your notice eye-catching so that it will be read? What do you want from your notice? If you are calling a meeting make sure you have all the details of time and venue correct. Do you want people to sign, call or email you?

E-mail

Is this is an effective way to discuss an issue with a colleague? Perhaps some reply quickly and relevantly while others ignore your email completely. It's a good is way to communicate but can be a big timewaster too. It's easy to start the day by downloading emails which are then answered. Sending those leads to more emails and so on. Do they dominate your life? How can you organise emails to benefit from their convenience while not letting them take up too much of your time?

Good communication is vitally important in the workplace. Unless you communicate clearly with colleagues, with patients and their relatives, then part of your effectiveness is diminished considerably. How well do you connect with others? Have you ever asked for feedback? It is often assumed that doctors have a good '*bedside manner*' naturally. There are ways to improve communication skills. The first step is becoming aware of yourself and how you communicate. Communication is a two way process. It's about giving out and receiving. It's about listening and about talking. It's about understanding and accepting. It's about acknowledging and valuing.

Perhaps you are frustrated by colleagues who don't understand you? Is it as much you who doesn't understand them? Do you listen to what they say and really hear and understand their concerns? Notice how often you jump to a conclusion when someone has just started to speak to you. If you want others to understand your point of view then the first step is to start to understand theirs much better. Do you listen to their concerns? When you do that, you will often find that they can hear yours too.

A big step forward in improving your communication skills is being able to explain to others what's bothering you. So often you may be assuming that the other person is able to read your mind. Unless you explain, he or she may not be able guess what you are anxious about. Are you uncomfortable talking about yourself? You could start by listening more intently to them.

Really listening. Deeply listening. Listening for what is not said as well as what is said. Listening for emotions too. The more you become interested in them, their lives and their problems the more they will tell you and the more likely it is that they will eventually listen to you too.

What stops you doing whatever would be the greatest help to you? Do you avoid the conversation you need to have, about finding it difficult to cope, because you are anxious about their reaction? Do you worry that you will be considered useless if you admit some vulnerability? Do you wonder about your references if you complain about the situation or say that you are not prepared to put up with it any more?

You may have felt for a long time that your situation is intolerable and yet you continue to tolerate it. What is stopping you making the changes you want? Do you say that you can't alter the system? That's true but you can make the system more bearable. Are you waiting for others to take the first move?

When will you realise that for something to change you have to do something different yourself? You have to make the decision, then and there to take some action. One of the most effective ways to start the process of change is by having a conversation with the people involved. You have to listen as well as to talk. You have to understand others as well as yourself and to explore creative ways to do things differently.

Communicating more effectively

Call a meeting. Is there a way that you can meet with your colleagues, if you have concerns about the running of the department, or have suggestions for ways to improve it? You could ask for an item to be on the agenda to bring the matter to the others' attention.

Have your say and make sure your opinion acknowledged and considered. Notice if there a hierarchy in your department. If so and you are senior, listen to the views of the juniors instead of dismissing their views. If you are junior make sure your opinions are heard.

We have two ears and one mouth to listen twice as much as talk!
If you have an issue is for discussion about a change or improvement how quickly can you consult your colleagues? Are they open to different ideas? Are you?

Dr. X a specialist registrar dreads out-patient days. The list is always twice as long as the recommended optimum length as recommended by the College. She finishes the clinic exhausted and frustrated about there being nothing she can do about the situation. She starts to think about how the outpatient list is filled. She hands a slip which says 'six weeks' to the patient. The booking clerk books the patient for the appropriate clinic however many names are already on the list. What is the basis of the decision to see the patient after six weeks? Why not twelve weeks? Twenty-four weeks? Do they actually need a follow up appointment, or is this 'the routine'? Could they be given guidelines and asked to call in for appointment if certain symptoms occur? (i.e. the responsibility of care is handed to the patient) With some trepidation, Dr X brings this topic to the next departmental meeting.

To her surprise there is unanimous agreement from the consultants and registrars that the situation is intolerable for them too. The outcome of the discussion is that the clerks are told to inform the doctor when the clinic is fully booked so that a decision about when the patient will be seen can be made.

Dr. X looks forward to her clinic and her colleagues thank her for initiating this simple change in procedure. (see also Chapter 17 for more on this)

Be clear about:

- what you prepared to do
- what you not prepared to do
- what your colleagues expect of you
- what your specific role is
- how flexible you are prepared to be
- when you will you say no

Maintain standards

What are your standards? Decide how you want your department or practice to run? What is important to you in your working environment? Is there something that your colleague does or doesn't do which irritates you? Have you discussed this with them? (Communication again!)

Dr A. believes his partner Dr. B isn't doing her fair share of the work in the practice. He resents her being part time. He thinks she should be doing more on call. He doesn't discuss this with her and is very irritable whenever he speaks to her. Because they are so busy they only talk to each other when they pass in the corridor at the surgery. Dr. B finds the situation unbearable. She wants to leave the practice but her husband encourages her to stay because it is convenient to where they live and there are no vacancies advertised locally. She tries to be all things to all people: a perfect doctor, mother, wife but the strain is beginning to show. She asks Dr A to set aside an hour for a meeting to discuss these issues. She decides what she wants to achieve from their meeting. She wants to be clear about what he expects from her in terms of on call and time in the surgery. She wants him to understand that she would like to leave on time at the end of the day so she can pick her child from school. She suggests several options to enable this to happen and to do her share of the work. She prints this and gives it to him to consider, before they meet. The outcome is that they understand each other much more. They come to an amicable agreement and their working relations improve.

You can make a difference. Have a conversation!

Chapter 17: How to see less patients in your clinic

A clinic day

It's another day. Your heart sinks. You dread finding out how many patients are waiting to see you. You know that the day is totally unpredictable and you will be handed a fully booked list with another name or two squeezed in. This won't represent who actually attends the clinic because some will fail to arrive at all and others will be added as last minute emergencies. Some will come who have nothing at all wrong with them because they don't want to let you down, doctor.

How are you?

Can you feel your blood pressure rise as you walk towards the outpatients or into your surgery? Do you feel the beginning of a stress related headache? Do you say to yourself yet again: *'I can't stand this situation much longer.'* Are you fed up complaining? Do you grumble bitterly to anyone who will listen that there is no way you will put up with another busy clinic? Have you decided enough is enough? You know you can't carry on with the stress. Something will have to give. And it may be you.

It's always the same

Nothing changes, unless it's for the worse. You get there, take one look at the list on your desk, groan inwardly and wonder how you'll ever get through them all. *'it's the system'* you say *'I can't change the system'*

Are you relieved when several patients fail to arrive? Do you dread that one day everyone might turn up and you wonder what you would do? You know the system is near breaking point but believe that you are powerless to do anything about it. But is that true? What can you do to improve this state of affairs? Everyone you speak to shrugs their shoulders and tells you not to complain. That's the way it is. Stop making a fuss. You count yourself lucky you're not working in the hospital on the other side of town. The doctors there have to see twice as many patients as you. So, you take a deep breath, swallow a paracetamol or two and push the buzzer for the first demanding patient who storms in complaining that she has been waiting for over an hour.

Ask yourself

- why every clinic is overbooked
- who decides it's OK to go over the designated limit
- who actually makes the appointments
- how the appointments made
- how many are new patients, how many follow ups
- what the interval is to see a patient again
- what is achieved from seeing a patient at an arbitrary fixed time interval
- whose needs are satisfied
- rationale for the time interval between visits

If you are doing what you've always done don't be surprised that you get what you've always got. Perhaps now is the time to start to think about the situation differently. Can you picture a clinic which begins and finishes on time? What options have you got for this to happen in your clinic?

An ideal clinic

- how many patients
- time designated for each
- ways to ensure appointments were kept
- criteria for follow up visits
- emergency provision without disrupting everything
- way to lessen the number of emergency visits

Start by imagining, in your mind's eye, what an ideal clinic would be. See yourself there now. Picture it. Listen to it. Hear the calm voices. Feel the relaxed atmosphere. (Difficult, but keep trying!) Imagine yourself, with a smile on your face. You are unruffled and stress-free. You arrive at your bright and airy consulting room filled with sunshine and fresh flowers to find a neat list with exactly the number of patients booked which your College recommends. There are a couple of vacant appointment times for any emergencies or for patients anxious about symptoms they have.

Smiling patients are seen at the correct time of their appointments. They too are tranquil and serene. They discuss with you and are fully involved in their treatment options and each patient away fully understands both your role and theirs in the management of their medical condition. All patients leave your consulting room pleased and are heard to say something along the lines of *'Thank-you doctor. I will do whatever I need to do so that the treatment you've prescribed will work in the very best way for me'*

At the end of the clinic, you do a ward round and complete your correspondence before having a delicious healthy lunch in the beautiful hospital restaurant. You are happy and know that you have done a good morning's work.

Then the alarm goes off and you wake up. It was all a dream. But does it have to be? What can you do right now which will help you towards making this dream a reality?

If you write down the answers to the questions below, brainstorm, draw a mind map, decide to take some action then you may find that the action of one or two people can make a difference.

- How can your patients be more involved and responsible for their treatment and well-being? There is a subtle difference between telling someone they have to give up smoking and asking them: '*What do you need to do differently to help you recover?*'

- Do your patients know and understand their illness so that they recognise which symptoms to look out for?

- Do you provide a telephone number and a time they can call to talk to you if they are concerned about their condition? A few minutes on the phone to you may relieve their anxiety and prevent another appointment being used.

- When you've finished with someone in your outpatient clinic, you hand them a piece of paper to take to the desk to book their next appointment. Ask yourself, do they need to be seen again as a routine?

- Have you reviewed with your colleagues the reasons for seeing patients as follow ups? What is an optimum time? Why six weeks? Why not four weeks, eight weeks or six months? Do you want to know if they have developed signs or symptoms? Do you need to see them if they feel well? Could any tests be done without taking up clinic time? Could they be told the result by telephone, e-mail or even via the Internet?

- Talk to your colleagues about the routines in the department? Have a creative discussion to explore other ways of practice.

- Be prepared to listen twice as much as talk to find imaginative solutions.

- Draw up new guidelines.

When you change things you and your colleagues arrive for the out-patient clinic, look at the patient list and feel relaxed about the next hours ahead.

What will you do now to take more responsibility for a lasting change in the system, to make the dream a reality?

Assumptions allow the best in life to pass you by.   John Sales

Chapter 18: The end of the road or a new beginning?

When I retire I'm going to spend my evenings by the fireplace going through those boxes. There are things in there that ought to be burned.
Richard Nixon

How do you feel about reaching the official end of your everyday life as a doctor? Perhaps you've been considering ways to keep in medical employment after retirement.[47] But how do you look on the idea of giving up medical work? Do you see it as the end of the road or a chance to do something entirely different? Will it be a time for closing down or opening up for you? Have you always expected to retire when you are 60 or 65 but noticed that your workload and the nature of your job have changed so much that it is more of a chore than a joy? Would you like to retire but feel a bit scared at the prospect?

There's no doubt about it: practising medicine is a fulfilling profession. But if it has taken most of your time and energy for years the thought of never seeing another patient may fill you with joy tinged with panic. When you no longer have the stress of it all, will you miss it? You may say you can't wait. But deep inside you have a lurking doubt. You know that you'll miss being a doctor and wonder what to do instead.

Which of your needs are fulfilled by being a doctor?

A doctor has status in the community. Being a doctor is great for your self esteem: your opinion is valued and respected. You have security too, both financial and personal. There is also support: in theory, you have supportive colleagues who will encourage you to progress within the medical profession and achieve your career goals. If you want to meet any or all of these four needs then it's important to consider how you will do this outside medicine.

---

47 Lewis J. Continuing working after retirement age. *BMJ* 2002; 324 S163

Think about your life

It is the end of another long day and you've finally arrived home exhausted. Perhaps your briefcase is full of work to do before you go to bed. You've got years to go until you're officially due to retire. Have you planned how you'll spend your days when you are no longer doing busy clinics, long operating lists, or endless surgeries?

Do you reassure yourself: *'No problem. I'll take a few weeks' holiday and enjoy myself. I deserve a rest after all those years of being overworked'?* Is the rest of the plan vague or have you some specific things that you'll do?

Whether it's your choice or someone else's, you may experience a gamut of emotions when you finally decide to take the plunge. You may feel a sense of sorrow, sadness, anger, and guilt; a period of grieving for a part of your life that is over.

Your new life

Eventually you will be ready to move on to your new life, as *'a doctor retired from clinical practice.'* What do you imagine this will be like for you? That may depend on your attitude and motivation and how you plan to use your time. For some people it will be too easy to do nothing except be a couch potato. For others it will be a chance to discover that there are a multitude of fresh doors along their corridor of life waiting to be opened.

Starting your new life

Can you look forward to this part of your life as the start of something new and exciting? It will be a chance to do things you never had time to do while working as a busy doctor. It will be a possibility to increase your skills, to learn something, to discover a talent, or to travel to destinations both outside and inside yourself. Whatever takes your fancy, this is the time to make your dreams into reality.

Don't simply retire from something; have something to retire to.
Harry Emerson Fosdick

Why wait?

Perhaps retirement is still a long way off for you. What's stopping you making changes currently? How about living some of your dreams now, making sure that your needs are fulfilled by activities outside as well as inside medicine.

Dr X found time to play the piano regularly when he decided to stop bringing work home with him in the evening. How did he do this? He stopped putting papers in his briefcase at the end of the day. The next morning, he felt refreshed when he returned to his desk to do the tasks.

Can you find a way to start doing what you want in parallel with your medical life? What's stopping you? It is possible to be a doctor and have a life too.[48]

Another kind of gardening

If you start to plant the seeds of your intentions for your retirement today, you will have taken the first step towards nurturing your new life. Just like your garden, you may keep on doing little bits, but you may not see much happening immediately. The following summer, however, you will be able to enjoy all sorts of amazing shrubs and flowers. The seeds you plant now will ensure that one day you'll be able to enjoy a happy and fulfilling retirement, whenever that may be.

We must be willing to let go of the life we have planned, so as to have the life that is waiting for us. EM Foster

---

48 Kersley S. Striking the balance. *BMJ* 2001; 323 S2-7325

PART FOUR

Case Studies

Disclaimer: The following 'case studies' are based on general situations experienced by many doctors. None relates to a particular individual. Any resemblance to a specific person is purely co-incidental.

Too many people, too many demands, too much to do; competent, busy, hurrying people-it just isn't living at all.
Anne Spencer Morrow Lindbergh

Chapter 19: It's all too much

Presenting Complaint

You are a busy GP. It's the beginning of another week. You dread going to work. You are always exhausted. The day is never long enough to do everything you plan. It's always the same. From the moment you walk through the door of the surgery, you are bombarded with requests to sign forms and answer queries. There are phone calls which may result in extra patients to be fitted into an already busy clinic. There will be aggressive patients demanding that something has to be done and telling you pointedly that they know their rights. There are an enormous number of repeat prescriptions to sign, with not enough time to review whether all the medication is absolutely necessary. At least those patients aren't filling appointment slots. What is soul destroying is the situation never seems to improve. You used to think it was just a 'bad week' and the next one would be better. Now you realise, with a sinking heart, this is it. This is what it's like to be a GP in UK society today. At least this is what it is for you.

There are a few colleagues who seem to be coping well. From your perspective it's difficult to understand how they manage to keep a cheerful expression. They even seem to be able to have a game of tennis on their half day and have been heard to mention they went out at the weekend with their wife and children. As far as you are concerned these sort of things are almost forgotten luxuries. There's too much to do, always, to even consider any leisure activities. Your partner doesn't understand however many times you've tried to explain how important your work is that it has to take priority over anything else and he or she should have understood what living with a doctor would be like.

However, you don't think you can cope with your life as it is much longer. You don't sleep very well any more and have been overeating and drinking more alcohol than you know is good for you. As a doctor it's very difficult to know who you can turn to, who you can talk to about how you feel. You believe that everyone else apart from you copes well. You know you have to deal with whatever life throws at you.

History

You have always been a caring person and want to make a difference to people's lives. Because you were good at science at school, your teachers encouraged you to do medicine. It's been a rewarding career both financially and emotionally until the last few years when you've wondered what it's all about and begun to feel very disillusioned with it all. You have always enjoyed the intellectual process of coming to a diagnosis, treating your patients and the satisfaction of seeing them recover. However even that enjoyment has disappeared recently. You are fantastic at caring for others but have neglected to care for yourself. These days you find it difficult to remember why you entered the medical profession. What you do all day bears little resemblance to your dreams of life as a doctor.

Examination

Outwardly you look well, even though somewhat tired. Your partner nags you about your weight. You believe that as far as the patients are concerned, you manage the workload adequately if not extremely well. Your patients seem to love you, although there have been a few complaints recently which you believe is the climate of increasing litigation towards doctors rather than any personal failing in your ability to practice adequately. You are smartly dressed and exude an aura of confidence. You rarely show any irritation with your patients or colleagues.

Home life is becoming rather stressful. When you eventually arrive, you meet an irate partner and a cold supper, and you tend to have a short fuse. Your family relationships are suffering. Inside you are in turmoil. You know this situation isn't right and that it can't go on much longer. You have some anti-depressants in your bag and wonder whether to take them.

Investigations

You need time to think about what has been happening lately. Find a quiet place to do this. Yes it seems impossible but your life depends on you changing the situation. Here is what to ponder: what are the most important areas of your life to you?

Place the following in order of importance to you: career, family, close relationship, friends, community, spirituality, self care, money. Is the order related to how you actually spend your life? Isn't it time to get your priorities right? Do you neglect your own needs as you look after those of your patients? When did you last do whatever it is that you love to do? What can you do for a few minutes as a start, something which will give you a buzz, make your heart sing again?

Write down your thoughts and re-read what you've written several times and consider them carefully. How are you going to change things?

Diagnosis

Chronic overwhelm

Treatment

Prescription for Change

Don't wait for the system to change. You have to take action to do something for you and your life.

You **can** make a difference by changing yourself. The important thing is to start. Today. Begin by doing something, anything, differently. If you don't know what to do, clear your desk or throw away the pile of journals that you won't ever have time to read. Let go of believing you might miss reading something important. If it's that important it will appear elsewhere or someone will tell you about it.

Take time to sit quietly to think about and imagine your ideal life, in your mind's eye. Be aware of what you see, hear and smell. What does that feel like? What small steps are you prepared to take to move towards this dream? Decide on a very small action and get going with that today.

For example: here is a way to stop interruptions while you are seeing patients.

Specify a period when you do not want to be interrupted by phone calls or persistent queries. How much time will you start with? Half an hour? Ten minutes? Two minutes?

Explain to the receptionist and the others in the practice that from now on you are unavailable for any interruptions during the specified time.

Instead of continuous or random interruptions you could instead designate a specific period of time for requests, phone calls when you will be available for patients and others. In this way the caller can be told when to phone you. During these times, be open and willing to be there for them.

Start to say 'no' when asked to do something extra which you don't want to do. Decide what you are definitely not going to do any more. Then without getting into any discussion about why just say 'no' and mean it. When you say 'no' to something, what are you saying 'yes' to?

Think about to whom you can assign some of the routine tasks. Delegate more. Get others to do the non medical stuff. If necessary employ an extra assistant for this. Don't make any more excuses about why you can't do that. Make a start today with something, however small.

Shift the situation, bit by bit, day by day, until you make a complete recovery. You **can** change, just be willing.

Prognosis

Excellent, if the prescription is dispensed soon.

A Challenge

Imagine you are the doctor described. What will you modify to reduce your actual or potential overwhelm? What has, or is stopping you make those changes? What small adjustment can you make tomorrow to make you life better?

Chapter 20: The consultant

Presenting Complaint and History

After years of struggle, long hours and endless studying for higher exams you arrive, at last, at the golden destination. You reach the pinnacle of your medical career; the prize you strived for is yours. You are a hospital consultant. However, even though you are highly regarded by both your patients and your colleagues, you feel let down by the long hours of work, by the lack of support from the system, and by the frustrations of inadequate facilities. You also have nagging doubts about not being good enough, about being a fraud, about not being quite ready for this. Although being a consultant is no longer, necessarily, a job for life, the appointment feels like a life-long commitment, a life-long sentence. Not only the job but all that goes with it: is this the place you really want to live in for the next thirty years? You don't want to be saddled with the massive mortgage. You want to have the time to do fun things, the things you promised yourself you would do when you could afford to. Now that you can, in theory at least, afford them you haven't the energy or excitement any more

Was it for this that you worked so hard? Has it been worth the sacrifices? You neglected your friends, your family and your own well-being along the way. You've survived the arduous journey and reached the place you dreamt of and now wonder if it is the right destination. You have a demanding private practice as well as an everlasting NHS list of patients waiting to consult you. You are the person with your name over the patient's bed. The responsibility stops with you. The threat of litigation is like a little gremlin sitting constantly on your shoulder, shaking a finger at you and reminding you to do the extra test to be sure that every eventuality is covered. Life is more stressful than ever. You are far too busy to take any time off, so when the holiday times are arranged you end up working over Christmas and at other times you would like to have as time off. You always pull the short straw because you are the most junior consultant.

You are in demand to speak at International meetings about your latest research, so conferences have to take the place of holidays. It's more stress for you but you dare not say no. Your colleagues tell you that you have to join the circuit. That it's important to build your reputation.

It goes on and on. Years pass. The work load increases. Even at weekends, you keep on working. You see private patients and operate late into the night to boost your income to pay for the house and the private school fees. Your spouse comments that you look tired but you ignore this and tell yourself that you can cope. You convince yourself that this way of life is only short term and yet the pressure continues. You know that you will have to slow down and take a holiday. But nothing changes. When you take a few days off, the workload accumulates so much while you are away that you dread going back afterwards.

Sometimes you think, very fleetingly, about retiring early. You do the sums and come to the conclusion that you have to work until you are sixty five because of the heavy financial commitments you have. On the other hand you wonder what you'll find to do with yourself. because work is everything. There is nothing else in your life. Even though you complain, you realise that your life will be empty if there was no work to fill it.

Rather alarmingly you notice, then ignore,   occasional chest pains recently felt, when you are particularly rushed or stressed. Luckily you have some ancient glyceryl trinitrate tablets which you found at the back of a drawer. You take one if the pain is bad and tell yourself you have indigestion. You don't have any time to see your own GP, even if you had one. Why should you, when you know what's wrong? You never got around to registering when you moved to this city when you were appointed as consultant. There seemed no point back then as there were always colleagues around to have a quick word with after meetings. But deep down you are scared.

As your reputation and private practice grew, so too has your NHS load and the frustrations of the guidelines and targets to follow which bear little connection to clinical need. You are always too busy looking after others to have time for any self care. You vary between missing meals completely and eating large restaurant meals with pharmaceutical reps when negotiating funding for your latest research project. Exercise is a word you relate to books rather than moving your body. You convince yourself you are fit enough as you get in and out of your car to do clinics in different hospitals. Your family seems to inhabit another world into which you rarely enter.

Examination

What's happened to you? Would you want to be treated by someone who is as tired and drawn as you? You see a face in the mirror of someone exhausted and stressed. Where has your joy for life gone?

Investigations

Wheel of Life

Draw a circle and divide it into eight equal segments. Label each:

- career
- money
- health
- friends and family
- significant other/partner
- sprituality and personal growth
- fun and recreation
- physical environment

The eight sections in the Wheel of Life represent the state of balance in your life. The centre of the circle is zero score, the circumference is a score of ten. Indicate your level of satisfaction in each area of your life by drawing a line across at the appropriate point within the segment. Your line does not have to touch those in adjacent segments. Which part of your life needs the most attention? Are you having a bumpy ride? Do you like the situation? Note your answers and consider them carefully.

Diagnosis

Extreme lack of self-care.

Treatment

Prescription for change

Start with self care. Mind, body and spirit all need nurturing. Since all aspects of your life are interconnected you have a choice: consider how to increase your fulfilment in the areas of you life which you ignore at the moment. Think how to make the best parts of your life even better. For example, if you improve your self care by eating healthier food, your general well being will improve and you will enjoy your work more

Prognosis

Excellent, if the prescription is dispensed and taken soon. A little change for the better each day can lead you to complete recovery.

Suggestion

Look after yourself much, much better. What can you do today to improve your physical and emotional well-being?

- eat healthily
- stop smoking
- limit alcohol
- take regular exercise

Whatever you decide, '*just do it*.' Decision without action is pointless. Find someone to make changes with you: a friend or a coach to support and motivate you through these changes. Indulge yourself. Don't make any more excuses about why you can't do this. Make a start today with something, however small.

Challenge

Imagine you are the doctor described. What will you change to improve your self care? What has, or is stopping you make those changes? What can you do differently today to start to make your life better?

Action may not always bring happiness; but there is no happiness without action. Benjamin Disraeli

Chapter 21: The doctor's wife

The doctor's wife…must realize proudly that her husband is in the privileged class -privileged to have duodenal ulcer, coronary thrombosis, and a lonely life. She must   never be jealous, a virtue that harks back to the pre-stethoscope days when the doctor laid his bearded face on the lily-white bosom and listened with one ear for rales and with the other for the patient's husband. She must be sympathetic with her husband, for no one else ever will be. Earle P. Scarlett

Presenting Complaint

You are a doctor's wife who wonders what is happening in your marriage.

History

Life as a doctor's wife turned out differently from what you imagined. You met and fell for each other as students. Your friends envied you so much. You longed to have the status of 'doctor's wife,' but over the years the reality has changed. You moved so many times because he was on rotations which involved hospitals far apart. This meant that your own career was curtailed. Your children attended several different schools. You find it increasingly difficult to make social contacts each time you move. Your husband is always working. Your social life is virtually non-existent because he either has an emergency to deal with at the time you are going out or he comes home too tired for anything. You wonder what happened to the considerate person he was when you were a staff nurse and he worked on the same ward. Now you wonder whether he fancies the night sister more than you. When he is at home he expects everything to be organised around his needs. He is used to telling others what to do and his requests being carried out. You hardly remember you used to run a ward full of desperately ill patients. Many of your friends in similar situations have divorced and you wonder if your marriage is doomed too. You feel as though you have to keep things together for the sake of the children. You are too busy looking after them, your husband, your home and fitting in your job as practice nurse, to have any time for your own needs. Most of the time you can't even remember what your own needs are. You have forgotten who you are.

You don't know what's happened to your life or the dreams of a wonderful life.

Examination

You are an intelligent creative person with so much potential which has been lost in the 'doctor's wife' role. There are parts of you which remain in embryonic form, even though you are a mature adult.

Investigations

Do you look after own needs as well as you look after those of your husband and children? When did you last do whatever it is that you love to do? What can you spend time doing for just half an hour a week, to nurture yourself?

Diagnosis

Relationship deterioration

Treatment

Prescription for change

Take time. It's not too late to make some changes. Successful relationships depend on various factors. One of these is clarity of boundaries. It's important to say 'no' and mean it when you don't want to put up with something any more. You **can** be a person in your own right in spite of, or as well as, being part of a couple or a family. Do what you love to do. Sometimes this will mean visiting friends or going out to the theatre or cinema with them or on your own. If you make a start things will improve for you. A little each day can lead you to complete recovery. You will find again the person hidden beneath the role of doctor's wife. Is now the time to fill the gaps in your life?

Prognosis

Excellent, if the ***prescription for change*** is dispensed today, and the first steps taken urgently.

Challenge

Start to look after yourself much, much better. What can you do today which will improve your physical and emotional well-being? Practise saying 'no' this week to things you no longer want to do. Take time to do something you really enjoy. Remember what it felt like before you were a 'doctor's wife' and try to recapture that feeling again. Find someone to support you to make the changes: a friend or a coach to encourage you. Go on, indulge yourself!

Don't make any more excuses about why you can't do this: make a start today with something, however small.

If you are the doctor's wife described, what can you do to improve your life? What has, or is stopping you? What change, however small, or large, can you make starting today to make your life better?

If you are a doctor, married to someone like the person described: recognise that she is also a person. Recognise who she is beyond her role.

Chapter 22: Impending burnout

Presenting Complaint

You feel worse each day. You are more and more tired and irritable. You don't want to get up in the morning and have little motivation. You wonder what life is all about. You've been drinking more alcohol than you used to do, but convince yourself that you can stop at any time, no problem. You know you'll have to seek help one of these days but worry about confidentiality. You believe that whoever you see locally will talk to others and you don't know how to find someone to consult in another area. You have thoughts about ending it all if things don't improve soon.

History

Since going to medical school your whole identity has been encapsulated in the role of 'doctor', which has taken over your life. Every waking hour is filled either by the endless work or worrying about what you did, what you should have done or what you would do next time. Your self esteem is at rock bottom. Work is the only thing in your life. It has priority over everything else: your self care; your friends and family; your relationship with your partner; your spiritual needs and community. Patients with chronic diseases and others who don't recover return to you over and over again, so you have a distorted view of your success. It's easy to forget you have cured and helped more people than your 'failures.' You believe those who don't recover reflect your incompetence. This leads you to working longer and longer hours with less time for other things.

Examination

Exhaustion. Classic signs and symptoms of a carer who cares for everyone but forgets about him/herself. You are a healer who needs healing.

Investigations

Answer the following questions: When did you last have a proper lunch break, with food and a time away from the work? If you had a day off what would you do for yourself? When did you last have fun? A good laugh?

Diagnosis

Build up to Burn-out

Treatment

Prescription for change

Don't wait until it's too late. Make some changes. Answer the questions and start to take action today. If it's difficult to do on your own, talk to a friend, partner, colleague or coach: someone you can trust to support and encourage you. Don't delay. Stop the process before it builds to full blown burn out.

How can you start to care for yourself more?

What new boundaries will you put in place? Who will you say 'no' to? Think about this: if you were asked to do something extra at work which is absolutely vital, you **would** shift things around to find some time. Put your own self care in the same league. Free up time to look after yourself.

What will you do differently? A little each day can lead you to complete recovery. Make the start to fill the gaps in your life.

Prognosis

Excellent, if the *prescription for change* is dispensed today, and the first steps taken urgently.

You may delay, but times will not.   Benjamin Franklin

Chapter 23: Life is wonderful

Sometimes being a doctor dulls your positive emotions. What you are most likely to feel strongly is frustration, anger, resentment and depression. It's good to be tuned in to all sorts of sensations, the good as well as the bad, the positive as well as the negative. How would you like to feel wonderful more often? Would you question it if you were overwhelmed with a sense of joy, of exhilaration and excitement?

Presenting Symptoms

A yearning for a totally different life experience.

History

A couple of months ago you noticed an advertisement in the paper about a charity walk in the desert in Africa. You can't explain how reading this made something happen inside you. It was the antithesis of your *'ideal holiday'*. You would camp, not wash for a week, wear dirty clothes, purify your drinking water with iodine tablets and walk fifteen miles a day in hot and dusty conditions. Yet something about the advert spoke directly to you. It seemed to say: *'come on you can do it.'* You wonder if you are completely crazy. However the desire to take part has become a passion and you think about it day and night. You wake up with vivid dreams of what it might be like. You spend every free minute planning money raising ideas, a get fit schedule, and making lists of what to take with you (and surprise yourself being able to find a few free minutes).

Examination

You are a person with a mission. There is the beginning of a sparkle in your eyes and a faint sound of your heart trying to sing.

Diagnosis

Charity challenge fever.

Well done getting this condition. It will benefit not only you but also those others you inspire to do the same. (If you haven't caught this yet find someone who has and try to get infected)

Treatment

Prescription for change

Stop making objections and be convinced that you will succeed.

When you next see a poster for a challenge decide to take part, put aside any objections which come into your mind. Keep asking yourself: what is the worst thing that could happen?

Prognosis

Excellent, if you let your spirit lead you. Taking part in a challenge is wonderful. You will feel on top of the world. Some of the benefits of taking part:

- learn about the charity and what it does
- make a significant contribution to their funds through fundraising activities
- take the training seriously and become much fitter
- gain a sense of community with the other participants
- work as a member of a team helping one another
- have a spiritual experience

The night sky in the desert is like twinkling black velvet; and the vastness of the sandy plains and rocks: an enormous vista as far as the eye can see is an amazing feeling. You feel on top of the world, content, happy and exhilarated.

When you complete a challenge you **know** you can do **anything**.

So what challenge will you take? Take a look at www.atd-expeditions.co.uk This company organised the charity trek I completed in the Namibian desert. The organisation was superb. They specialise in treks for various charities all over the world caring for the participants, the environment and they support local conservation projects.

Challenges are what make life interesting; overcoming them is what makes life meaningful. Joshua J. Marine

Chapter 24: Uncertainty

Presenting symptoms

You want to make changes but don't know what.

History

You are at a turning point in your life. There has been much pressure on you from your boss to follow a particular career path. You are looking at an application form for a sought-after job but it isn't what you really want to do. Friends and colleagues tell you not to be so silly. You are the favoured candidate and this is an opportunity not to be missed. You know it doesn't feel right for you. You wonder whether to stay in your profession or leave.

Diagnosis

Unsettlement about what to do next.

Treatment

Prescription for change

Make a decision and follow it up.

What is important in life? What do you love to do? What can you do to bring that into your work? If you stay in your present job what could you do to improve things? Have you talked to your colleagues and told them how you feel? If you go to the new job what would be the benefits to you? What would be the disadvantages? Imagine yourself in your existing job in a year. How will that be? How will you feel? Do the same for the new job?

Which appeals to you most? What other options do you have? Take a big sheet of paper and write down every possibility you think of, however outrageous.

Drawing a mind map is helpful. Put the words *'Where to now?'* in the centre and then draw lines coming from this leading to your options. From each word other things will occur to you. See what happens and what links with what.

Go for a walk or sit quietly and listen to yourself. You will become aware of the answer that is right for you. It's your life: only you know how to live it.

Food for thought

You want to make changes in your life but don't get around to doing anything about them. What is that about? What's stopping you? What is the worst thing which could happen if you did what you want? Are you prepared to *'get out of the box'* and think about your situation differently?

Imagine how you would like your ideal life to be. Take one very small part of this and introduce it into your life now. Start to behave *'as if'* all is as you would like it to be. Other changes will start to happen. If for example, in your ideal life you would go swimming once a week, then fit in some swimming now even for half an hour every two weeks.

Everyone who is overworked and putting up with a bad situation, may hope that someone out there will change things. It feels easier to stay in familiar discomfort than to take the big step, the leap into the unknown, so have the courage to say *'enough is enough'* and make the changes yourself otherwise nothing will ever change.

It's time to find some creative solutions to the situation you've had enough of. Start with first steps to make it happen. Become very clear what you will no longer tolerate and come up with ways to change these. Then even the seemingly insurmountable can be overcome.

Chapter 25: Professional exams

Presenting symptoms

You spend every hour of every day trying to revise for your professional exams. It's bad enough being on call and working nights. You are zombie-like because of chronic lack of sleep. Coping with all that, do you need the stress of taking your higher professional exams too?

History

The date of the exam is looming and you believe you will never finish all the studying you think you need to do. You spend hours each day sitting at your desk, book open until sometime later realise you've fallen asleep. You design complicated revision plans but regularly fail to keep to the strict regime you've set for yourself. You are not sleeping well and start to panic. You don't want to fail the exam but convince yourself this will happen. You are a perfectionist and expect to know everything.

Treatment

Prescription for change

You think you know nothing and will fail again. Take a reality check: is that really true? Who is this exam for? People like you who have been working in the speciality for a few years who deal with the day to day challenges.

Ask yourself, you failed before. Was it to do with your exam technique rather than your lack of knowledge? You know many of the answers, perhaps you haven't presented them the way the examiners want them. How can you improve your technique? Is your handwriting legible? Do you plan your answers for a few minutes before you start to write? Do you divide the available time so that you have enough to write something for each required question?

Tips for Re-sitting Exams

Would you like to pass next time? What can you do?

Change your attitude

Believe in yourself. Indulge in positive self talk: from *'I don't know anything'* to *'I know enough about this to pass this exam'*; from *'I am nervous'* to *'I am confident'*.

Look at your body language

Are you slumped in your chair, shoulders rounded, arms folded with a sad expression? Sit up straight with your shoulders back and put a huge smile on your face. How does that change the way you feel?

Practical suggestions

Here are some things you can do.

- look through old papers
- list the subject headings and tick them off as you revise
- do essay plans: one a day you will have five by Friday
- expand one each week into a full essay
- reward yourself
- ask for constructive criticism from a colleague

Very few people achieve 100% in an exam. Even the examiners say this is impossible! You don't need to know it all to succeed. You have to be good enough not perfect.

What will be useful?

- a broad knowledge of the subject
- a good exam technique
- ability to plan your time to answer the required number of

questions
*   positive self talk

Good luck for the next time!

Is this a metaphor for other parts of your life?

Let go of your need to be perfect. Relax. Life always offers new challenges. You can never know it all. Don't despair. You will always know something. Work out where and from whom you need help or support.

There is one piece of advice, in a life of study, which I think no one will object to; and that is, every now and then to be completely idle - to do nothing at all. Sydney Smith

Chapter 26: A New Year story

It's the end of the conference dinner. Most of the meal has been taken up with the man opposite and his colleagues talking shop. It's the one thing they have in common with each other. It's like an ego building exercise. They vie with one another to suggest that each one has more stress than the next and more difficult dealings with the management. They all deplore the lack of money for their department and the rules imposed from faceless politicians. It's as though whoever made mention of anything else might lose credibility. How could they possibly be doing their work properly if they had time for other activities? Not unexpectedly this belief means that the members of this group work obsessively long hours and always find reasons why they can't do what they used to, years ago. It seems almost as though work is used as an excuse they use, not to face challenges in other parts of their lives. I'm bored with all the specialist talk. I decide it's time to break the mood, to open up the conversation a bit. I smile across the table. The tired man opposite me smiles back and looks surprised.

'How are things with you?' I ask.

'Can't wait to retire. Only another couple of years.'

'What will you do then?'

'Oh the usual. Buy the boat. Potter around on the river. Take it over to France.'

'How come you are waiting until you retire? What's stopping you doing that now?'

'Busy. Much too busy. You've no idea. Targets. Management decisions. Possible litigation. I'm completely exhausted by the time I get home. Couldn't possibly start going out on a boat then.' He sighs deeply and looks at me.

'Actually I do understand. I retired early from medicine. I wanted to do other things. I encourage others now. Do you realise that if you really wanted to, you could start to sail a bit even now. There's no need to wait until you retire. You just have to make a start.'

'Maybe you're right. My poor old colleague had his retirement all planned out, then, blow me down, a month after the farewell party he had a stroke. Uses a wheelchair now and he can't do many of the things he planned. Never know, do we, we just never know what's around the corner.

Do you know what? What you said has really got to me. Suddenly decided what to do. I'm going to buy the latest edition of the boating magazine and look at the adverts. Yes, I'm going to buy that boat next week. I can hardly believe what I'm saying to you, but I know I'll do it.'

'Here's my number. Do give me a ring in a couple of weeks and let me know what's happening.'

A few weeks later he phones me.

'Listen it was all very well you persuading me to buy the boat but I still haven't any time to sail it. So what do I do now? I'm not sure whether I need whatever it is you offer. You know I feel awful saying this: I've been a great success all my medical life and yet I can't seem to get myself organised enough to get out in this fantastic boat. I'm extremely busy so would find it difficult to find the time to come to see you.'

'Let's arrange a time to talk. This way we can both assess whether we could work together to achieve the changes you want to make. By the way I work on the telephone so finding time for coaching needn't be a problem. Freeing up time is something we can work on, if you wish!'

He phones at the appointed time. I ask him to spend five to ten minutes telling me about himself and how he would like his life to be.

He tells me he is in his early fifties, married for the second time and is a surgeon in a large district general hospital. He feels undervalued and overworked. He hates the added administrative work and the pressures to reach targets. To get the work done he has to start his operating lists or ward rounds early in the morning so leaves his house before his children are up.

His ward rounds are extremely long because he is terrified of litigation so is obsessive about checking everything. His temper is shorter than it used to be and he knows that he gets unduly annoyed with the anaesthetist and the theatre staff who remind him at the end of the day that they want to go home.

He arrives there after seeing his private patients, his children have gone to bed and his supper has dried out. He is too tired to talk to his wife and the last thing he wants to hear about is her day or her problems. It's a lifestyle he's been following for years.

'So do something with that,' he laughs cynically down the phone line.

I ask him to tell me what his life will be like if he carries on as he is doing. He groans and tells me he thinks he'll probably end up with a heart attack.

Un-phased I ask him who 'he' is apart from the surgeon.

'If you could look into the future at yourself living a wonderful life, what would you see there? Where would you be? What would you be doing? What would you feel like?'

There is silence for a few moments.

'Very interesting questions. You certainly are making me think. I can hardly remember who I am apart form the surgeon bit of me. I used to enjoy painting years ago, oils and so on and when I retire I plan to learn how to sail and go off at weekends up the river or along the coast. Something to do one day. I've made a small step towards that by buying the boat'

He pauses for a moment then adds,

'Do you know sometimes I wonder if I'll ever reach retirement, or if the stress of this life will kill me before then.'

'What do you do to care for yourself? Do you take any exercise? Do you eat healthy food? Do you spend time in nature or wherever makes you feel calm? What do you do to relax?'

'I joined a gym last year in January, new year resolution to get fitter and lose some weight. Waste of money, that was. Only been there a couple of times and now a year has gone by. You are right about nature. I'd much prefer to walk in the country or even cycle than go to a gym. If only I wasn't so busy at work.'

'Do you know something about 'systems theory'?' I ask him. 'This suggests that all the aspects of our lives are interconnected. If you change one part others change too, almost effortlessly.'

'Tell me more'

He sounds interested.

'Well the best way to understand is to try it,' I laugh. 'What change could you make this week to make a start? Forget about work for the moment. We've been talking about self care. What small thing would you be prepared to do this week to look after yourself better?'

'Exercise. I like the idea of riding my bike. Yes, I'll do that. I'll take my folding bike to the hospital and ride around the grounds in the middle of the day. Instead of having a big lunch I'll take some sandwiches, and go over to the park opposite to eat them.'

'Anything which might stop you doing that?'

'Well there may be a lunchtime meeting with a sponsored lunch. I may not get around to taking sandwiches from home'

'That's OK. So, what can you promise to do?'

'I will promise to have a bike ride three times in the next week. I'll buy sandwiches in the canteen, so don't have to waste time making any.'

'Excellent. How long do you plan to ride?'

'For fifteen minutes each time.'

'Great'

I ask him to tell me what value he's had from our conversation and if he has any questions.

'I was very cynical; I'll be honest with you. But even during this short conversation I realise how powerful your questions are. They certainly made me think. I feel much supported. I know the suggestions came from me. What you asked got me thinking. I found the answers inside myself. I feel very focussed now.'

Within three months he is sailing each week. The relationship with his wife has improved and he sees his children regularly.

When we meet again at the conference dinner the following year I hardly recognise him. He looks fit and well and greets me with a big smile. As we shake hands he tells me. 'Talking to you last year was like a catalyst. I've certainly changed my life since then. I can't express the value of that to me and my family. It's been my best year yet.'

PART FIVE
Life coaching for change

Without change, something sleeps inside us, and seldom awakens. The sleeper must awaken. Frank Herbert

If we don't change, we don't grow. If we don't grow, we aren't really living. Gail Sheehy

It is not necessary to change. Survival is not mandatory.
W. Edwards Deming

Chapter 27: **Let your heart sing**

To find the universal elements enough; to find the air and water exhilarating; to be refreshed by a morning walk or an evening saunter ... to be thrilled by the stars at night; to be elated over a bird's nest or wildflower in spring - these are some of the rewards of the simple life. John Burroughs

What lies behind us and what lies before us are tiny matters compared to what lies within us. Ralph Waldo Emerson

Stop and listen

What does the voice inside reveal to you? It is telling you what you want very much. Can you hear what it says above the roar of your day to day cacophony? Would you like to open your heart to living a life you really want? Which door did you close when you opened the one to become a doctor? What would you find if you opened it again?

Is your life too routine, too busy and too stressful? Are you engulfed in the day to day overwhelm of general practice? If you continue along the same path what will you regret if or when you reach the age of ninety five? Have you forgotten what it's like to have fun, to have a laugh?

You don't stop laughing because you grow old. You grow old because you stop laughing. Michael Pritchard

Do you want to do something wild and wonderful? Is your answer a *'don't be so silly'* or *'what would people think of me'*?

Would you love to:

Re-visit hobbies, play music, sing, walk, jog, paint, write, dance or photograph or whatever, but believe you don't have the time?

Are you scared to feel that almost forgotten buzz again from doing something really exciting? How about trusting your instinct, your inner voice, which urges you to give something a try? You may say *'....what if I fail? What if they think I'm crazy...?'* Have you tried reassuring yourself with a *'never mind that...at least I had a go!'* ?

Whose life are you living? Are you sure? Who sets the agenda you follow?

How can you change?

1. Daydream

To accomplish great things, we must dream as well as act.
Anatole France

Close your eyes. Imagine being at one with the universe, at ease, happy, fulfilled, relaxed. Who are you? What are you doing? Where are you? How do you feel? What's different?

2. Listen

What gives you, an extra-ordinary sense of excitement, a buzz, an awareness of *'this is what life is about'*, that you need more of again?

3. Believe

Has your life as a doctor suppressed your natural creativity? Is it the right time now to allow your imagination to run free? What beliefs about yourself or the 'system' stop you having a fabulous life? Are you scared of what others might say or think? Is that the way you want to live? You can't predict how the other person will react if you behave differently. They, like you, have a choice. You may even be their inspiration if you start to *'walk your talk',* if you actually do what you've been dreaming about for ages.

Change your thoughts and you change your world.
Norman Vincent Peale

4. Do it your way

To live a creative life, we must lose our fear of being wrong.
Joseph Chilton Pearce

Has the time come to put **you** first for a change and *'feel the fear and do it anyway*[49]? Is **now** your opportunity to have what you want in your life?

5. Get out of your rut

Find a rope to haul yourself out of your hole and seek whatever support and encouragement you need to change your life.

It's not that some people have willpower and some don't. It's that some people are ready to change and others are not. James Gordon

6. Keep going

Your decision and enthusiasm to make a change will give you momentum. Decide your goal. Be pro-active. Work out the steps to get there and you'll be well on the way. Keep going and you will get to where you want to go.

7. Hold on

Julia Cameron[50] recommends two wonderful tools to keep you on track. These are *'morning pages'* and taking yourself on an *'artist's date'*

Every day cover at least three pages in your journal with flow of consciousness writing, write your thoughts about what's happening and your reaction to the changes you're making or just write rubbish. Think of morning pages as a limbering up exercise for your mind.

For your artist's date, make a commitment to do something on your own, just

49 Jeffers, Susan *Feel the fear and do it anyway* 1991 Rider
50 Cameron, Julia *The Artists Way* 1995 Pan books *The Basic Tools* pages 9-24

for you. This could be, for example, an outing, a walk, or sitting quietly in the garden.

8. Take action

If you really want more joy and happiness then truly believe in yourself and know that you have the power to create the life you want. Stop waiting for others to do things differently. You can change your life yourself[51]. But you have to do something. You have to take the first step, however small.

They always say time changes things, but you actually have to change them yourself. Andy Warhol

9. Keep going

Do I hear you murmuring 'been there, done that, started a load of projects but can't stick at anything'? What can keep you going? Will you use your diary, a computer programme and charts to tick? Who can be there for you? Someone who will encourage you to do what you want and give you positive encouragement? Your partner, friend, relation, mentor or coach? Someone to travel along this bit of your life's journey with you for a while?

Go confidently in the direction of your dreams. Live the life you have imagined.   Henry David Thoreau

10. Celebrate

What will you do when you are on the top of your world?

I celebrate myself, and sing myself. Walt Whitman

---

51 Covey, Stephen *The 7 Habits of Highly effective people* 1999 Simon and Schuster

Chapter 28: What on earth is Life Coaching?

Go confidently in the direction of your dreams. Live the life you have imagined. Henry David Thoreau

Do you sometimes wonder what life as a doctor is all about and whether the satisfaction and enjoyment from it is balanced by the stress and overwork?

Have you ever thought about or questioned whether acclaim from your colleagues is worth the time physically and emotionally away from your family, your partner and most important of all, yourself?

Within the chapters of this book you've been encouraged to think of ways to change so that you truly can live the life you want, both as a doctor and as a human being.

You've been challenged, among other things, to find more time,[52] look after yourself better,[53] stop procrastinating,[54] communicate more effectively[55] and improve your personal relationship.[56]

The fundamental messages

- it **is** possible to make changes for the better
- define your specific goals
- recognise and maintain boundaries
- clarify personal responsibility
- say 'no' if you don't want something
- start big tasks with small manageable chunks
- explore different ways to find solutions

52 Kersley, S What would you do if you had the time? BMJ 2002 324(7334): p. 53S

53 Kersley S Looking after number one   BMJ 2002 324(7338): p. 85S

54 Kersley, S Do you procrastinate? BMJ 2002 324(7348): p. 164S

55 Kersley, S 'Do your colleagues understand you?' BMJ 2002;324 117

56 Kersley, S Relationship: what relationship? BMJ 2002 325(7361): p. 60S

- take action

So far, so good. Perhaps you really **do** want something different in your life and yet a year on you are in the same place. You are as frustrated as you were and think that you have to put up with it all. Consider what your life would be next year or in five years, if you continue in the same way. Is it more comfortable to stay in your discomfort than to take a risk and do something different? Are you ready to step out of your comfort zone?

What are you waiting for?

Are you waiting for someone else to take the first move? What's stopping you being pro-active? Is it fear? What are you frightened of? What's the worst thing that could happen? If what you fear happened, what would you do? Are you letting that stop you?

It helps to have someone on your side. Who can support you and give positive encouragement? Is there is a friend or a member of your family who can do this[57]? If they are part of the problem, or have their own agenda which might discourage you, perhaps you could ask a mentor or a coach for objective encouragement.

What is coaching?

The term 'coaching' with the prefix of 'life', 'personal,' 'executive,' or 'corporate,' is said to have been coined by Thomas Leonard[58] in the early 1990s. The model comes from sports coaching. The principles and philosophy of coaching incorporate the ideas of Maslow, (self actualisation) Lucke and Locke (goal setting) and Steven Covey (seven habits).
It is about:

- believing in possibilities
- being accountable

57 Lagnado, M Friends and family are good (and cheap) life coaches BMJ 2002 324(7345): p. 1099a
58 Thomas Leonard 1956 - 2003

- challenging assumptions
- having a sounding board
- being motivated
- having a catalyst for change
- devising strategies
- thinking creatively
- setting and achieving goals
- being action orientated
- considering different options
- deciding which action to take

What are some of the tools coaches use?

- non-judgemental listening
- open questioning
- brainstorming
- mind mapping
- positive affirmations
- visualisation
- goal setting
- action steps
- journaling
- encouragement

What is the difference between coaching, counselling and mentoring?

There are similarities and connections between all of these.

- **Coaching is about moving forward** from where you are in your life to where you want to be.

- **Counselling is for understanding** and coming to terms with your past, support to contain and movement out of a crisis situation.

- **Mentoring is guidance** from someone, in the same speciality who can advise, encourage and support you in your day to day work.

Coaching doctors and others

Coaching is widely known within the business Community. *'....it bridges the growing chasms between what managers are being asked to do and what they have been trained to do...'* [59]

Even in the British Medical Journal, coaching has been discussed, described or mentioned in the recent past. [60] [61] [62] [63] However within the medical culture there seems to be a reluctance to seek support even when it may be required.

Dr A was pleased when colleagues noticed not only his desk was clear and tidy for the first time in living memory and also he was less stressed and listened to them much more effectively. He asked for their opinion instead of trying to enforce his own ideas. Even his wife noticed he was better company. He was reluctant, however, to admit that the changes had happened after he worked with a coach.

Who is it for?

You, if you are a successful consultant, GP, hospital or community doctor who is overloaded by the demands and challenges of your profession. In spite of the fact that you look after your patients faultlessly something is missing in your life. You wish you felt the enthusiasm you had when you first qualified. Perhaps you believe that it would be difficult to make life better so you carry on and you neglect yourself and your needs, your partner,

59 Morris, B, So you're a player. Do you need a coach? Fortune magazine 21 February 2000 Vol 141 No 4 p 144
60 Atik Y, Personal Coaching for senior doctors BMJ 2000 7240 Vol 320 S2
61 Philp Ian, ...and Ian Philp describes the sensation of being coached BMJ 2000, 7240 Vol 320 S2a,
62 Hutton-Taylor, Sonia Cultivating a coaching culture BMJ 1999, 7188 Vol 318 S2
63 King J, Dealing with difficult doctors BMJ 2002 Vol 325 S43

your family and your community. It seems easier to stay where you are instead of making the changes you want, and yet there is a little voice inside telling you that life doesn't have to be like this.

It is possible to be a doctor and have a life too
Coaching is a catalyst for change

A journey of a thousand miles begins with a single step.   Confucius

AND FINALLY

Life is like a spreadsheet: when you change one thing everything else automatically changes too.
Susan E. Kersley

Appendix 1: Frequently asked questions

How do I find a coach?

- Use search engines for 'Life Coach'
- Personal recommendation. More and more people are hiring coaches these days. It's a good way to find anyone from a plumber to a coach. If you've experienced coaching which you found useful, don't keep it a secret, recommend your coach to your friends and colleagues.
- International Coach Federation: www.coachfederation.org
- Coach University: www.coachu.com
- Coachville: www.coachville.com

Why hire a coach?

If you are ready to make changes in your life but lose interest and enthusiasm when things go wrong, you may want someone unconnected with your day to day life, onto whom you can bounce ideas. A coach will listen, ask questions to make you think, and help you find the way forward. A coach has just one agenda: yours.

Does a coach tell me how to solve my problems?

No. A coach enables you to find your own answers. Deep inside, you already know what to do, but something stops you doing it. You can talk to your coach about what's stopping you and come to realise that it's possible to face up to and overcome your fears in order to achieve what you want.

What happens if I contact a coach?

Most coaches offer a free introductory discussion so that the two of you can decide if you would benefit from working together. You will get a sense of what coaching is, and whether it might be useful. You also have the chance to ask the coach any questions you may have and for the coach to explain how she or he organises the sessions.

I live in a small town

Most coaches work on the telephone so it doesn't matter where you live. Choose a coach who seems right for you.

What happens next?

If you decide to proceed, then the coach will tell you how they work. Some require you to sign on for a minimum time; others leave it to you. If you are responsive to coaching you may make big changes very quickly. However it's useful to make a commitment to at least three months coaching if you want lasting change to occur.

The coach will send you an intake form or questionnaire to help you focus on what you want to achieve. You may also be asked to complete in a *'call preparation form'* before each session.

How are the sessions organised?

This varies according to the individual coach. Sessions may be from half an hour or longer. You can make big shifts even in a relatively short time. A challenging question can change your life! By the end of the session you will have promised to take some action before you speak to your coach again.

How much does it cost?

What would living a better life be worth to you?
Coaches charge professional fees.

Recommended reading

Leonard, T. **The Portable Coach,** Scribner 1998
Whitlow, J. **Coaching for Performance,** Nicholas Brealey, 2002
Whitmore and Sandahl. **Co-Active Coaching**, Davies-Black 1998
Covey, S. **The Seven Habits of Highly Effective People,** 1992
Covey, S. **First Things First,** Franklin Covey Co 1994
Miedaner, T. **Coach yourself to Success,** Contempory Books, 2000
Richardson, C. **Take time for your life,** Broadway Books 1998
Forster, M. **Get everything done**, Hodder and Stoughton 2000
Hay, L. **You can heal your life**, Eden Grove Editions 1988
Jeffers, S. **Feel the fear and do it anyway** Rider 1987
Cameron, J. **The artist's way**, Pan books, 1995
Buzan T. **The age heresy** London: Ebury Press, 1996
Macnab F. **The 30 vital years: the positive experience of ageing**
Kiyosaki RT. **Rich dad poor dad,** Warner books, 2002

Resources

The Open University www.open.ac.uk
The Open College of Art www.oca-uk.com
University of the Third Age www.u3a.org.uk

Appendix 2: The International Coach Federation

The information below is reprinted from the ICF website, www.coachfederation.org, with permission.

What is the International Coach Federation (ICF)?

The ICF an organisation with more than 4,000 members and 177 chapters in 31 countries. It is the largest worldwide non-profit professional association of personal and business coaches and provides Professional, Master and Internal Corporate Coach certifications. It establishes and administers standards for credentialing professional coaches and coach training agencies.

Coaching is an interactive process that helps individuals and organisations develop more rapidly and produce more satisfying results. Coaches work with clients in areas including, but not limited to, career, transition, life/personal, executive, small business and organisational/corporate. As a result of coaching, clients may set better goals, take more action, make better decisions, and more fully use their natural strengths.

What is the ICF Philosophy and Definition of Coaching?

The International Coach Federation adheres to a form of coaching that honours the client as the expert in his/her personal and/or professional life and believes that every client is creative, resourceful, and whole. Standing on this foundation, the coach's responsibility is to:

- Discover, clarify, and align with what the client wants to achieve
- Encourage client self-discovery
- Elicit client-generated solutions and strategies
- Hold the client as responsible and accountable

What is the definition of Coaching

Professional Coaching is an ongoing partnership that helps clients produce fulfilling results in their personal and professional lives. Through the process of coaching, clients deepen their learning, improve their performance, and enhance their quality of life.

In each meeting, the client chooses the focus of conversation, while the coach listens and contributes observations and questions. This interaction creates clarity and moves the client into action. Coaching accelerates the client's progress by providing greater focus and awareness of choice. Coaching concentrates on where clients are today and what they are willing to do to get where they want to be tomorrow.

Is there an ethical code for coaches?

Here is the Pledge of Ethics by an ICF Member Coach:

As a professional coach, I acknowledge and honour my ethical obligations to my coaching clients and colleagues and to the public at large. I pledge to comply with ICF Standards of Ethical Conduct, to treat people with dignity as free and equal human beings, and to model these standards with those whom I coach. If I breach this Pledge of Ethics or any ICF Standards of Ethical Conduct, I agree that the ICF in its sole discretion may hold me accountable for so doing. I further agree that ICF's holding me accountable for my breach may include loss of my ICF membership or my ICF certification.

What are the ICF Standards of Ethical Conduct?

I will conduct myself in a manner that reflects well on coaching as a profession and I will refrain from doing anything that harms the public's understanding or acceptance of coaching as a profession.

I will identify my level of coaching competence to the best of my ability and I will not overstate my qualifications, expertise or experience as a coach.

I will, at the beginning of each coaching relationship, ensure that my coaching client understands the terms of the coaching agreement between us.

I will not claim or imply outcomes that I cannot guarantee.

I will respect the confidentiality of my client's information, except as otherwise authorised by my client, or as required by law.

I will obtain permission from each of my clients before releasing their names as clients or references.

I will be alert to noticing when my client is no longer benefiting from our coaching relationship and thus would be better served by another coach or by another resource and, at that time, I will encourage my client to make that change.

I will avoid conflicts between my interests and the interests of my clients.

Whenever the potential for a conflict of interest arises, I will, on a timely basis, discuss the conflict with my client to reach informed agreement with my client on how to deal with it in whatever way best serves my client.

I will, on a timely basis, disclose to my client all compensation from third parties that I may receive for referrals of, or advice given to, that client.

I will honour every term of agreements I make with my clients and, if separate, with whoever compensates me for the coaching of my clients.

I will not give my clients or any prospective clients information or advice I know to be confidential, misleading or beyond my competence.

I will acknowledge the work and contributions of others; I will respect copyrights, trademarks and intellectual property rights and I will comply with applicable laws and my agreements concerning these rights.

I will use ICF membership lists only in the manner and to the extent that I'm so authorised by the ICF or the applicable ICF Chapter or ICF Committee.

I will coach in a manner compatible with the ICF Definition of Coaching and, whenever asked by my clients about my ethical standards, I will inform them of my pledge and agreement to comply with the ICF Pledge of Ethics and ICF Standards of Ethical Conduct.

What people say about my articles in the British Medical Journal:

You're certainly doing your bit in raising the level of awareness of life coaching amongst UK doctors with your refreshing series in the BMJ. Just read the latest and was inspired to send a rapid e-response!

I loved this article, as usual! You are really developing a wonderful style in your writing... YOU are beginning to shine through! You write in a lovely informal style that is clear to understand and you make the point succinctly.

Another great article!

This is excellent Susan - you go from strength to strength. There really are no accidents in this Universe - you are perfect to be the person who introduces doctors to coaching. I love your writing style and the way you make coaching palatable to the medical profession.

Another excellent one! You've really done a service to your community!

I have had a look at the article - another absolutely brilliant one - encouraging me to get going on my stuff.

Thank you!! I also wish you continual ongoing successes with your fabulous writing, perhaps we'll see a book by you, I hope so, because it will be a good one.

I loved this article, as usual! You are really developing a wonderful style in your writing... YOU are beginning to shine through! You write in a lovely informal style that is clear to understand and you make the point succinctly.

I wish Susan the best of luck, keep up the entertaining articles, and to the doctors I will say that whether it's other people telling you or you know it yourself, it's time to take the steps to improve your life. Rather than anaesthetising your own difficulties, there are other ways to bring more options and choices into each and every aspect of your life. Ask Susan.
Well done, Susan! A truly excellent and inspiring piece.

What a great article! I'm sure those who read this article are eagerly awaiting your next - or are wanting to be your clients. This approach is so badly needed in the caring professions where everyone is under so much pressure to give more and yet more.

Well done, Susan... another practical, down to earth article which really focuses in on the problems doctors must face. I am sure lots will draw much benefit.

Good succinct stuff. I'm trying to execute some of your ideas, they all make very good sense.

What can I say but ABSOLUTELY FANTASTIC!!!!!!

Thank you for the glorious work you're doing! Your articles are full of inspiration for all of us who have ever been associated with the medical profession!